GREAT
SALES
GREAT
LIFE

GREAT SALES GREAT LIFE

The Hidden Power of "The Ripple Effect"

Donald J. Noone

amacom

American Management Association

New York • Atlanta • Boston • Chicago • Kansas City • San Francisco • Washington, D. C.
Brussels • Mexico City • Tokyo • Toronto

This publication is designed to provide accurate and authoritative information in regard to the subject matter covered. It is sold with the understanding that the publisher is not engaged in rendering legal, accounting, or other professional service. If legal advice or other expert assistance is required, the services of a competent professional person should be sought.

Library of Congress Cataloging-in-Publication Data

Noone, Donald J.
    Great sales great life: the hidden power of "the ripple effect" /
Donald J. Noone.
        p.   cm.
    Includes bibliographical references and index.
    ISBN 0–8144–0259–3
    1. Selling.   I. Title.
HF5438.25.N66   1995
658.85—dc20   94-45494
                                                        CIP

Printing number

10   9   8   7   6   5   4   3   2   1

To my family:
Rosemarie, Don, and **Seth,**
who give me a resounding
"Yes!"
every day

Contents

Preface

I am a salesman. I am self-employed and have sold my own services since 1974. I had to learn how to sell because in the beginning, I started out with a blank slate; I had no connections. I knew that there was a need in the marketplace for what I had to offer, but I also knew that no one was going to beat down my door and beg me to do a program for them. I read; studied; attended seminars on how to sell; listened to tapes; developed a prospect list; started the cold calling, the appointments, the presentations; and got the jobs. I even got to the point where I could teach others how to sell. I also got my share of disappointments, rejections, cancellations, and big deals that were in the bag, yet evaporated. I have jumped with joy at some contracts, and cried at some others. So, my dear brothers and sisters in the fraternity, please know that despite my academic credentials, I have been there—on the firing line. I want you to know that I understand the hard side of selling: the pain, the anxiety, the ups, the downs, the frustrations, and the pressures. I also understand the dark side of selling, where salespeople on occasion slip into the pit of bad attitude, lack of motivation, and loss of enthusiasm; become subject to distorted beliefs, fear, and unfocus; and fail to do what they already know how to.

I am writing this book for you, to show you some things that have helped me, and that hopefully will help you, too. My goal is to see you to become happier, healthier, more fulfilled, a better salesperson, and a person who sees beyond the occupation to the exhilaration associated with building a great life. So you are my primary audience, and I am going to teach you what I know about the *inner salesperson*. You already know how to sell; I want to teach you how to sell yourself *on* yourself, and challenge you with the prospect of uncovering the greatness that can be yours. I want you to see that selling does not exhaust your identity. It is only a part of your special destiny. I believe you are called to design a more encompassing special destiny; my job here is to help you find it.

Everybody Is a Salesperson

Although this book is addressed to professional salespeople—those who are already making their living selling a product or service—in fact, it is addressed to every man and every woman because anybody is a salesperson. What do I mean? Getting a sale is basically a process of persuasion. The salesperson is trying to effect a change, trying to move a prospect from a nonbuying state to a buying state; the task is to get a prospect to act in a certain way, i.e., to buy. Persuading someone to buy, to exchange money for a product or service, is really just a special type of persuasion. Since all of us spend a good deal of our time trying to influence other people to act in certain ways, a good deal of the time we are selling our ideas, ourselves, our proposals, our philosophies, our values. We are trying to get others to behave in a way that we find appropriate; we are trying to move them from point A to point B, to change them, to get them to go from ignorance to knowledge, from inaction to action, from doing this to doing that, from believing this to believing that. In other words, we are selling a good deal of the time and, unless we are in neutral, buying the rest of the time.

So although the focus here is, in the first instance, commercial, in the broader sense, this book is for everybody. The ideas, the values, the strategies, the recommendations go way beyond a commercial transaction, and are applicable to everybody most of the time. In my judgment, more joy, more love, more fulfillment, more zest, more fun, more passion with higher achievement, and more enriching experiences are what life is all about. Just as this book is designed to help salespeople move their focus beyond selling techniques to the real source of their success—their inner selves—it is, by extension, designed to help every reader get beyond the preoccupations of the moment to the energy and power within that can unleash creativity, growth, achievement, and enjoyment beyond the dimensions of the occupational role.

So, this book is my gift to everybody, not to salespeople alone. In it you will find the things that I have concluded make sense—the things I have used, still use, and believe can help you choose to take the steps that lead to a great life.

GREAT
SALES
GREAT
LIFE

Introduction

This book is about *yes* and the ripple effect. It is also about the principle of causality—any result that occurs is always preceded by a cause. Those results are either good or bad. Without ignoring the bad things that do happen, the focus here is on the positive things you and I can do that can result, as the title suggests, in great sales *and* a great life. Yes is the cause, and the ripples are the effect. The emphasis is on the need for you to say yes to all the important aspects of yourself and your life on this planet. When you do, this affirmation sends out positive reverberations in every other area of your life, and interestingly, those reverberations or ripples become causes that send out further ripples. So, a yes begets more yeses, and the ripples beget more ripples. This casual process can work for good or ill depending on whether the initial cause is a yes or a no. How to get more yeses in every area of your life is our challenge here.

A Word about Yes

On June 16, 1994, Lance Deal won the hammer throw at the USA/ Mobil championships, breaking the record of 268-8 set in 1988. On his second attempt, as soon as he released the hammer, he held his arms high and shouted, "Yes! Yes! Yes! Yes! Yes!" He knew. Intuitively he released these yeses because *yes!* is a word that expresses joy, fulfillment, celebration, affirmation. This is precisely why it is a theme throughout this book.

Yes! is also the word salespeople live to hear. A yes means the offer is accepted, the deal is closed, the sale is made. Everything a salesperson does is designed to get to that point in the relationship with a prospect. Even in the typical sales interview, the salesperson strives to get the prospect on a roll with a series of yeses to questions, all in preparation for the big yes. When it comes, the yes brings with it feelings of elation, joy, and happiness; a salesperson feels good about himself or herself, about the customer, about the world, and about life. A yes is comparable to a touchdown, a home run, a knockout, a win, a kill, a triumph, a coup, a record— whatever your favorite metaphor is. In selling, however, the emotional effect of the close is fleeting, and shortly thereafter the salesperson is out on the prowl again, to repeat the experience and the thrill that goes with it. Life thus becomes a hunt for the yes.

This book is about you, about your life, and about not only helping you get a yes to more and better sales, but, more importantly, getting you to give yourself a yes to having a great life. *Yes* is a word freighted with positive feelings; it connotes a sense of optimism. A yes is an affirmation of faith and hope that good things will happen in the future, and when good things do happen in the present, it is an exclamation signaling celebration. This book will point out the areas in your life to which it is necessary to give a yes. What those areas are is displayed in Figure 1, but first, a word about ripples.

A Word About Ripples

Picture yourself standing on the edge of a peaceful pool of water in a Japanese garden. In your hand you have a stone. You toss the stone into the air. It comes down and hits the water. What does the impact of the stone on the surface do to the water? It sends out ripples. The wavelike reverberations travel out to the farther reaches of the pool and disappear when the energy is expended.

A ripple is a consequence. A ripple is an effect. The cause is the impact of the stone on the water. The ripple effect is a metaphor suggesting that anything that hits the water will have reverberatory consequences. When the ripple effect is applied to a person, it means that a person is like a pool of water, and whatever has an impact on a person will have reverberatory consequences in everything that constitutes the person.

What are the major elements that constitute a person? They are feelings, self-worth, the mind, the body, choices, beliefs, problem solving, roles and relationships, experiences, and the universe

Figure 1. You and The Ripple Effect.

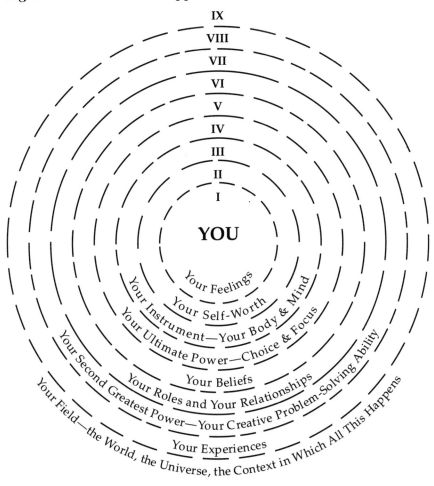

The graphic in its entirety symbolizes *you*. The *concentric rings* are the areas of life that have power to affect every other area; the *breaks between the lines* indicate the flow of impact from one area to another; the *ripple effect* is the dynamic consequence of causality, i.e., anything that occurs in one area of a person's life has consequences, for good or ill, in every other area.

or the context in which life is lived. To symbolize this interacting cause/effect relationship of one thing on another, I have created a simple graphic that reveals the areas of life that confront an individual (See Figure 1). The reality of life is that things experienced are meshed together, interlocked, reciprocal, and constantly in flux. Any analytical model, therefore, falls short of the reality. I recognize this; nevertheless, I want to separate the themes in order to talk about them and help you sort out what is often a mess, and such a mess that it impedes sales performance and personal happiness. I will also show you how they relate to the chapters ahead.

The graphic suggests where you start and how you proceed if you want to be a great person and a great salesperson. In fact, personal growth and development can start anywhere, but my contention is that for those already in the sales profession, the greatest payoffs will occur when the process of growth starts from the inside and proceeds outward in an orderly manner. Thus the sequence of chapter headings flows out of the graphic for the most part.

The first ring is entitled "Your Feelings." Feelings are fundamental ways in which energy gets expressed. They are at the core of the graphic because as long as you are conscious, you are feeling, and those feelings range along a continuum from ecstasy to depression, and every gradation between. Depending on the kind and intensity of these feelings, they can emancipate or enchain you. In many respects feelings are blind, which means they come as a consequence of something else. That something else might be beliefs, choices, focus, judgment, or behavior, for example. When these causes are negative, destructive, attacking, or self-defeating, you will get flooded with negative, depressive, or angry feelings, and the more these permeate your experience, the less effective, creative, innovative, and productive will you be. This, in turn, causes more negative feelings. What is even more debilitating is that the negative feelings then ripple through and color every other area of your life. Thus, you get caught up in a reciprocal rippling effect that affects every other ring adversely. The first chapter meets this problem/opportunity head on by showing you how to light the feeling fire within and send positive ripples throughout your being. You will learn how to turn the fire of enthusiasm on and up, how to use feeling power to deepen drive and motivation, and how to engage in appropriate behavior. Salespeople know the value of enthusiasm, but they often misunderstand its expression and crash when they fail. When confronted with disappointment, they often lose their enthusiasm, get flooded by bad feelings, and get caught in a downward distress spiral. Most do not know how to maintain enthusiasm in an ongoing way, or on command. This is the promise of the first and second chapters.

The second ring refers to "Your Self-Worth." Your self-worth is your intrinsic identity, your unique, ineffable essence, independent of roles, status symbols, and other external indices. It is at the core of vital energy and feeling, which overflow or are depressed, depending on the judgment you make about your self-worth. This self-worth judgment is where it all begins in terms of whether a person is in the business of pursuing happiness or pain (punishment). The self-worth judgment is so seminal that it has a rippling effect on every single aspect of your experience, for good or ill. You make this judgment in the early years of life (0 to 7), and it comes as a consequence of what the significant big people in your life have said to you. Fortunately, you can change it. If you have a negative judgment about yourself, it will instigate feelings and behaviors that will prove you are, indeed, inadequate. Conversely, a positive judgment about your self-worth will have an incredible liberating momentum that can enrich your entire life. The quintessential sale that salespeople need to make, therefore, is to sell themselves on themselves. Guidance will be given in Chapters 3 and 4 to help you do just that. The consequence will be a tremendous emancipation from limiting beliefs and a springboard to a new, transformed, powerful view of your self that will support outstanding sales performance *for the right reasons.*

The third ring deals with your instrument, which has two dimensions, the mind and the body. The most powerful dimension you have is your mind. If you do nothing to regularly renew it, sharpen it, focus it, as a salesperson, you will frequently find you are running on fumes. In Chapter 5 you will learn a mental renewal exercise that can lead to better health, inner harmony, personal centeredness, peace of mind, and explosive creativity. In the following chapter you will learn how to adapt this exercise to RAVE, an acronym for a most powerful reprogramming process that can not only fundamentally improve your performance as a salesperson, but change any other area of life you wish.

The other great dimension of your instrument is your body. To maximize available energy and provide a platform for optimum good health, a simple program of eating properly, breathing properly, and exercising properly is outlined in Chapter 7. You know that when you are sick, your productivity and the quality of your life erodes profoundly. Once again, physical health, or lack of it, will have a rippling effect on every area of life, for good or ill.

The fourth ring deals with the unique human power: choice and focus. When your choice is not on first things first, but on ninth things first, or some other low-priority matter first, the result will be adverse rippling consequences for yourself. Or if you believe that you have no choice, and your language is replete with "I can'ts," you have the key to a life of powerlessness and victimization. Getting in touch with this power and reorienting your life according to appropriate priorities will give you a sense of personal empowerment that may have been missing in your life. Flowing out of this belief in your empowerment is *focus*. It is not an exaggeration to say, "What you focus on will dictate your life." How to use this power to choose what you focus on and how to strengthen it will be explained in Chapter 8.

Along with the belief in the power of choice and focus goes the ethical dimension, which is treated in Chapter 9. All choices have a moral component that ranges from good to bad. Salespeople are not known to have exquisite standing when it comes to morals, e.g., honesty. The view in this book is that the only right kind of selling is ethical selling. In order to help a salesperson make proper ethical choices, an "ethics check" will be presented. It consists of three questions that can help you be on the side of the angels. The ethics check does not dictate the standards, but allows the salesperson to get in touch with his or her ethical traditions. Customers appreciate an ethical salesperson, and for most salespeople, doing the *right* thing has its own positive reward.

The fifth ring deals with beliefs. All the axioms about beliefs are true: "What you believe is what you get." "As you define it, so it is." Chapters 10 and 11 present life-enhancing core beliefs that can help you jettison much of the garbage that gets in the way of outstanding performance and the enjoyment of life.

The sixth ring suggests that being a salesperson is only one of many important roles you play, and, once again, whatever happens in one area of your life will have rippling effects, for good or ill, in every other area. Roles posit relationships. Guidance will be offered in Chapters 12 to 15 that can enhance relationships with others, whether the other is a spouse, a child, a customer, a relative, a friend, or anyone. How to communicate in a caring manner, how to deal with criticism, and how not to get hooked in go-nowhere games will be taught. When practiced, these techniques will help the people that enter your life feel special and help you deal effectively with the barracudas.

The seventh ring deals with another powerful capability that is profoundly underutilized by most people: *creative problem solving*. In Chapters 16 to 18 you will learn how to ask questions, how to enhance your creative imagination, and how to do quantum leap thinking and other solution-generating techniques. The reward for doing this will be that hitting and exceeding sales targets, no matter how ambitious, is a piece of cake.

The eighth ring deals with living, experience, time, your destiny—things over which you have control. Either life can happen to you or you can *make* it into something terrific. A strategy for putting your sales life into the context of building a great life will be developed in Chapters 19 to 21. Chapter 22 contains an efficient checklist that can remind you of everything you learned from the previous chapters.

The ninth ring on the graphic refers to your field—the world, the context in which your life unfolds. The world also can affect you for good or ill, whether it be recession, civil war, hurricane, tornado, the beauty of a mountain, a tender act of kindness done to you, or even an unexpected big check. The argument here is that everything that you have going for you in rings I through VIII will make the difference, in terms of either folding under adversity or growing more. It is important to note that the ninth ring has no boundaries, and points conceptually to the place where a person has a relationship to a superior being. I do not address this issue and only point out that the ninth ring is the field in which everything exists and that it permeates everything that exists. How a person deals with that concept can have important consequences, again for good or ill.

The Difference Between This Book and All the Other 261 Sales Books

The dominant focus of virtually all of the 261 books in print on selling is ring VI. (See Figure 2.) This figure highlights what is contained in most sales books. Their focus is on the sales role, and all the skills and techniques a person needs to master to be a successful salesperson. Most of them do touch on the other rings in passing, but few deal in any substance with what is referred to in rings

Figure 2. You and The Ripple Effect—sales role highlighted.

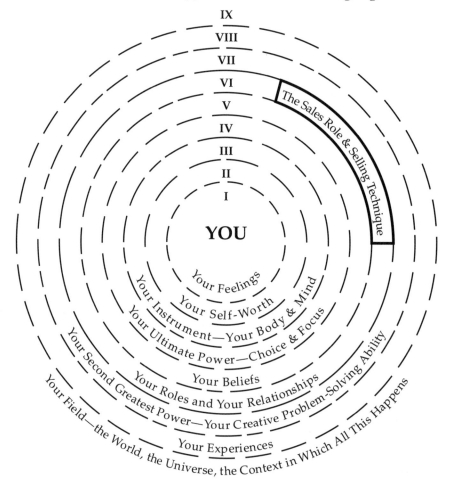

I through V and VII and VIII. As the graphic suggests, most of the books are narrowly construed and focus on technique. *Technique is not enough to be a great salesperson with a great life.* How to harness the inner salesperson and utilize the amplifying power of the ripple effect so that every aspect of your potential is actualized is what this book is about. Lest you think that this book is softheaded and has little to do with sales, I must say, *au contraire!* This integrated approach has everything to do with outstanding sales for the salesperson, because it creates positive energy, new ideas, and focus on the right things. Not only can it help you make a quantum leap in selling, but the joy of the trip will be unparalleled.

In conclusion, it is my hope that this book will lead you to outstanding achievement in sales, but all of this achievement, in my judgment, makes sense only when a life is well balanced with love, time to smell the flowers, enriching experiences, and personal fulfillment from a life well lived. If you read each chapter and do the exercises, I am confident that you will end up giving a resounding yes! to your life.

A Word About Format

The word that makes a salesperson's heart skip a beat is *yes*. Salespeople know that when they are interviewing a prospect and trying to move the prospect to buying, it makes sense to get him or her on a roll of yeses. Once a prospect starts saying yes to parts of a deal, the final yes is easier to get. You will notice that at the beginning of each of the subsequent chapters, there are three questions I want you to ask yourself. The probable answer to each one of the questions is yes. This disposes you to give a final yes to the contents of that chapter. In other words, my goal is to get you on a roll of yeses so that ultimately you will give an all-encompassing yes! to great sales *and* a great life for yourself.

At the beginning of each chapter, in the upper right-hand corner, you will also see a miniature version of the Figure 2 ripple graphic. It will have the concentric ring that relates to the chapter contents shaded. The reason for this is to reinforce the conceptual structure and add coherence to elements that are so often treated independently. In order to position yourself to reap the benefits of each chapter, study the graphic and answer the questions. It will be worth the investment.

1

The Fire Within

	Yes	No
1. Do you believe that you are on this planet to be happy?	☐	☐
2. Do you believe that it is possible for you to be happy on a regular basis?	☐	☐
3. Would you like to learn how to ignite the fire within on command?	☐	☐

Why is this chapter first? The reason is that I want to give you an instant return on the investment of your time and money in buying this book. That return is, in my judgment, the single most useful thing you can learn about life, about living, about selling, about being happy, and about enjoying the trip you're on. It is the one thing that will ripple through everything you put mind or hand to. It will make the reading of this book a joy. It will transform your relationships with the people in your life: customers, prospects, spouses, friends, lovers, children, and relatives. It will make you, without a doubt, an uncommon person on this planet. It will put you in the star category of salespeople. What is it? It is something so easy for you to have, so powerful, so energizing, so inspirational, so motivating, that you will wonder why you have not kept it on your front burner your entire life. But no one gives it to you, no one can make you have it—only you can bring it into your life. All that is necessary to have this incredible power ripple through your life, and make you feel alive and optimistic, is to want to have it.

Do you want it? Do you want to experience it? Do you want to find and use the key to transforming your entire life? I need a yes to these questions. What is it? It is enthusiasm! Nothing great was ever accomplished without enthusiasm. Enthusiasm is the fire inside, the passion that fuels drive, energy, and motivation. To tap into it, have it, and use it, you must understand what it is and what it isn't, and what it's like when you have it and when you don't have it. Most and best of all, you will learn how to bring it on instantly, intensify it, and make it a perduring influence that ripples through everything you consider and touch.

Enthusiasm operates at many levels, and at varying levels of intensity. At the most basic level, it is simply a feeling—a good feeling, a feeling of energy, a feeling of aliveness, a positive feeling. If we examine the Greek roots of the word, *en theos*, enthusiasm refers to the god within. It is an ancient word that refers to the spirit of the divine, the power that rules and permeates the universe, the divinity that is inside of each man and woman. Whether you believe in God or not, it can be understood at the very least as a metaphor for an incredible human power that can allow a person to do awesome things.

Let's look at the flip side first. If you get in touch with what it is like when you don't have enthusiasm, then it will be easier for you to appreciate it when you have it, or to bring it on when you want it. Think of the times when you have been sad, depressed, blue; when you experienced the blahs; when you were dissipated and could not focus—times when you were disconnected, at odds with yourself, and filled with guilt, remorse, frustration, disappointment, or feelings of failure and hopelessness. Think of times when you were in physical pain with a headache, backache, or injury, or when some virus or chronic disease had laid you low. The likelihood is that your feelings were deflated and flat, and you were experiencing self-pity, a sense of victimization, or even anger. If you can't recall ever experiencing any of this negativity, reflect on folks you know who have. Now, get a sense of what any or all of the states above were like. See them, feel them, reflect on them. You got it? OK. The likelihood is that you are in touch with a state that is devoid of enthusiasm. It is a painful state, a state of misery, a state that hurts, a state where a person is unfocused. Some folks live their entire lives from that perspective, and, as a consequence, little that is good or great occurs to them.

Other folks are so caught up in the pain that they search around for anesthetic to kill it. What are the favorite ones? Well, for salespeople they are smoking and drinking. They do indeed kill the pain for a while and provide relief from the ache, but the relief is always temporary. That is why those using these anesthetics always need another one. They eventually lead to addiction, and in the long term have profound adverse health effects. Other folks choose more potent, but just as damaging, substances, e.g., cocaine, heroin, or crack. Some choose paths that appear less hurtful, like cookie, TV, and sex addictions. All serve the short-term function of temporary relief, but invariably bring on greater pain, more guilt, more frustration, and more self-hatred.

This is surely a path we do not want to go down because it is at the opposite pole from the aliveness and joy associated with enthusiasm. Assuming that the path of enthusiasm is the one to go down regularly, the big question is, how do you get onto it, how do you stay on it, and when you drop off it, how do you get back onto it?

There are many ways to get into a state of enthusiasm, but the simplest way to be enthusiastic is to act enthusiastic. Frank Bettger wrote a classic book on selling that every salesperson needs to read, entitled *How I Raised Myself from a Failure to Success in Selling*. In the first chapter he recounts his early career as a major league baseball player. One day his coach said to him that his attitude was poor, he was lagging about like he was a twenty-year veteran, his spirit was dead, and he put a negative pall on the team. His coach told him he was sending him to the minor leagues, and that on the trip down there he should decide if baseball was really the career he wanted. While traveling to Johnstown, Bettger did decide that he wanted to play baseball and vowed to himself that he would become the most alive, enthusiastic sparkplug his new team had ever seen. In the next month Frank did exactly that; he was chattering all the time, ragging opponents, encouraging teammates, moving around the field with a vigorous display of energy. It became infectious, and the team, which was in the cellar when he arrived, moved up to first place in the league in eight weeks. In fact, his catalytic presence was noticed by reporters, and they gave him the nickname "Pep" Bettger. At the end of the eight weeks, his reputation reached his former coach in the majors, and they drafted him back. His ability as a baseball player did not change in those eight weeks. What did? His attitude, his beliefs, his feelings, and his behavior. Unfortunately, Bettger got injured, and that terminated his baseball career, but he concluded that if you really want to be a success at *anything*—baseball, selling, parenting, loving—you need to go at it with enthusiasm. On the last page of his first chapter, he highlights the point of this story, and I want to repeat it here for you: to become enthusiastic, act enthusiastic. The rationale behind this advice is that when you act, move, talk, gesture, and behave enthusiastically, messages from your muscles go to the brain, and the brain concludes, because you have given it a precedent at other times, that you must be enthusiastic. As a consequence, the brain opens up the biochemical pharmacy and stimulates the glands to secrete endorphins and other biochemicals that are the physiological support of that feeling state.

Professional actors know this, and I have discovered in my speaking that the act of speaking, even when I have begun the event physically sick, is such a tonic that I invariably feel better after the event. Why? Because when I am healthy and speaking, I am having so much fun that it is truly a high, and since I am practically always healthy, my brain, conditioned by the association of speaking with good feelings, believes that because I am speaking, I must be feeling great, so it opens up the biochemical pharmacy at its disposal and reinforces that feeling. That is the power of acting, that is the power of make believe, that is the power of changing behavior first, because then the feelings will follow.

That is the quick and easy route, something that is always at our disposal and is activated by a sheer act of our will. We just do it, and the results will follow. But to do it requires a decision to do it, a desire for a better state, and a strong desire to lift the self-imposed darkness. How can you dispose yourself to acting enthusiastically when you don't feel like it? Well, it's useful for you to ask yourself, when you are in a blue funk, "Am I on this planet to be happy or to be miserable?" If the answer is to be miserable, don't do anything. You've got it, and it probably will get worse. On the other hand, if the answer is to be happy, since there is no Santa Claus or fairy godmother who is going to come down the path, sprinkle fu-fu dust on your head, and make everything wonderful, then the rational question is, "What can I do to be happy?" Since enthusiasm and happiness are spins on the same phenomenon of feeling good, the answer is, *act enthusiastic!*

Now, since you know this is the path to enthusiasm, and since you know the payoff, one last propellant that I would put into your intellectual repertoire (and to quote myself) is this:

Do it now!
Do it when you don't feel like it!
Do it especially when you don't feel like it.

Now combine this with Frank Bettger's guidance. The new message would look like:

To become enthusiastic, act enthusiastic!
Do it now!
Do it when you don't feel like it!
Do it especially when you don't feel like it!
Just do it.

To make it easy for you, photocopy the message below. Blow it up if you can and put it everywhere as a reminder. Make a sign of it, and keep it in front of you at your work station, or put it on a three by five card over the visor of your car, or paste a Post-it note on your daily appointment book, or on your refrigerator, or by your bathroom mirror, and read it whenever you can. In no time at all you will see a tremendous transformation of your life and your relationships with others.

OK, that is the express route to changing one's feeling state. How can you make enthusiasm be a more perduring experience, and not so dependent on tricking the brain? The secret is to have goals you are wild about achieving. You show me someone who is depressed, blue, miserable, underachieving, disconnected, and without motivation, and I will show you a person who has no goals

---

How do I bring the joy of living into my life?

Become enthusiastic.

****

To become enthusiastic, *act* enthusiastic!

****

Do it now!

Do it when you don't feel like it!

Do it *especially* when you don't feel like it!

Just do it!

See the difference when you do.

---

about which he or she has a strong burning desire. This person might be among the homeless, the too comfortable, the couch potatoes, or even a good person who has built a life of safety and convenience. However, any objective observer would be able see that he or she is operating at about a tenth of potential or less. The person's life is dull, flat, and predictable, with very few peaks and valleys, and virtually devoid of passion. Why? Because he or she has chosen pain or comfort, and has abandoned any wish to max out on happiness. The way to maximize happiness is to have a goal or goals that you are passionate about.

How can people get passionate about something when they are not? First of all, if a person is to change, he or she has to want to change. Folks in their comfort zone typically don't want to change. And what happens? Nothing. Many kids in school don't want to learn, and what happens? The schools graduate illiterates. But what motivates a person to want to do anything? It is real simple—pleasure or pain, and strangely, people will do more to avoid pain than they will to reap the positive rewards that flow from some new course of action.

So how do you develop enthusiasm about something? First, reflect on the pleasures that would flow from having made a goal happen; see it in your imagination; feel it; imagine what others would say about your having made it happen. In your imagination, see the vivid picture of your having made it happen close up, panoramically, and of gigantic size, with movement and living color. Hold it in your mind, smile, and allow your body to get suffused with the good feelings of achievement. Suppose you have a sales target of $1 million in sales. Sit down with pen in hand and spell out all the rewards: the pleasures, the payoffs, the recognition, the applause, the good feelings, the monetary returns to you, the quality of life it could afford, the material things you could buy, and the exciting things you could do when you indeed accomplish it. This is left-brain type of analysis, and it's important for you to make explicit why you are going after the $1 million. Now, once you have filled up a page spelling out the payoffs to yourself in great detail, put the pen down and close your eyes. Rest in silence for a minute and take a few deep breaths. See the words stretched across a mountain top for a quarter of a mile in 100-foot-high uppercase Helvetica letters—$1 million in sales! While you're seeing it, say yes! with fists held tightly. Then bring the image up closer; put it in bright yellow, and then red, and then green, and then black, and then red again; and say yes! Hold those dynamic changing images in your mind for a minute. Then shift scenes, and now, with the movie-making capability of your creative imagination, in living color, run through in your mind's eye many of the big rewards on the payoff list you wrote out earlier. As you see yourself in these scenes, give yourself permission to feel great. When you capture that feeling, once again say yes! As you shift slowly from scene to scene, do it again and again. A number of profound consequences flow from this exercise if it is repeated daily. First of all, your feeling state gets elevated with elation, drive, desire, and motivation. The importance of this is that all the hard steps you need to take to make it happen now seem easy, like cold calls, planning an attack, preparation, etc. The images will not only dictate the feeling but support the execution, the doing. The great power of this exercise is that it helps you overcome inertia and gets you into action. Pretty soon the power of momentum takes over, and accomplishment is only a matter of time.

Often the pleasures flowing from a prospective goal are enough to turn a person on, but remember what I said: People will do more to avoid pain than to reap the positive rewards flowing from a goal. So you also need to get in touch with your pain. First, put your pen in hand again, and write down all the pains you will experience if you do not achieve your goal. In the example above, spell out in detail all the pains you will experience if you do not achieve $1 million in sales. All the rewards above evaporate. You slip into the faceless middle, or even wind up on the bottom of the heap. You're embarrassed; you feel guilty because you know you are capable of being outstanding. You put your job security in jeopardy—no company wants losers on board for long. Consider how others will think about you—those close to you, colleagues, friends, family. Get in touch with how depressed and miserable you will feel. Now make the pain vivid by associating the failure with swimming in a cesspool, or in wading up to your neck in a vat of vomit. Make these images vivid; see them, feel them, smell them, taste them, and be sickened by the thought of your choice to fail. When you have had enough of the pain associated with not achieving your goal, $1 million in sales, move back to the positive side of the ledger, and see yourself in your mind's eye as having made it happen. And reflect on the positive payoffs again.

Associating your failure to achieve with disgusting images may be repugnant, but if you are really interested in tapping your incredible creative imagination in support of your personal greatness, don't shrink from the exercise above, or be afraid to incorporate it into the process of creating a life you are indeed proud of. What you will be doing is tapping into the two things that will lift you aloft: the power of feelings and the power of internal visual pictures to motivate you to do the things you already know how to.

When you do this regularly in pursuit of your goals, you will find that enthusiasm is yours. Your walk will be different; your posture will be different; your voice will be alive; smiles will come readily to your face; "the incredible lightness of being" won't be just the title of a movie, but something you experience. And best of all, your dreams will come true!

Summary and Bridge

The fire within is enthusiasm. It is that incredible feeling power that can ripple through everything you put your mind to, if you want it. It is a power that can energize you into doing great things. Enthusiasm is a primal yes that comes from deep inside. It can be brought on, nurtured, amplified, and felt by the paradox that when you *behave* as if you have it, *bam*—you get it! By *acting* enthusiastic, you become enthusiastic; and by pursuing goals that are important to you, passion and enthusiasm will flow through you like a river. Thus, the goals engender enthusiasm, and the enthusiasm ignites desire and the will to act, which enable you to achieve your goals, which bring fulfillment, more enthusiasm, and more, and more—in a continuous upward curve of growth. Thus, when enthusiasm is linked up with goals you are passionate about (and this, incidentally, comes from being in touch with the pleasure and pain associated with those goals), it can become a deep, solid feeling foundation on which to build a great life.

The next chapter continues the discussion of feelings. Once you get a handle on this, the rest of the process of moving into the star category in sales and life is like dessert.

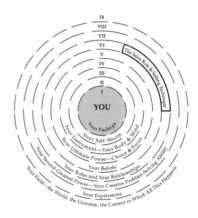

2

The Feeling Factor

	Yes	No
1. Do you want to learn what is the first mainline message to the brain that affects feelings?	☐	☐
2. Would you like to learn about the incredible role momentum plays?	☐	☐
3. Would you like to learn how to get into an achieving state whenever you wish?	☐	☐

The bottom line of life's experiences is how you feel. Everything you do, experience, or behold has an emotional consequence that will make you feel good or feel bad. Each person needs to decide whether he or she is on this planet to feel good and help others feel good, or to feel bad and help make others feel bad. I am on this planet to feel good all the time, and I would assert that that is why you are on this planet. The fact is, when you look around, you see many folks committed to being miserable and to making others miserable. How can you get to feel good all the time?

In the previous chapter, I explained how you can get into a good feeling almost instantaneously and make this a more perduring state by having goals you are passionate about. The ripples that enthusiasm sends out are all positive. It is truly an almost mystical power that you have at your fingertips that can transform everything you do. But what else can you do to take advantage of feelings, and what else can you do to be in a good feeling state all the time?

Physiology

Implied in the admonition to act enthusiastic in order to feel enthusiastic is a more generic path to sending messages to the brain, and that is the physiological path. Historically, when you have been happy, you smiled. When you felt good, you stood up straight and walked briskly. When you laughed, your brain thought you were cheerful. When you appreciated something someone else did, you clapped. When your team scored a touchdown, you jumped up and let out a yelp, or if you were in Arkansas, a souwee! When you were paying attention, you leaned forward in an anticipating posture. Conversely, think of the times when you were sad or blue, and remember how you held your body. Your head was hangdog low; your shoulders slumped; your muscles were soft and caved in; you held a frown on your face. These physiological expressions are counterparts to the feelings, and because of their historical association with the feelings, whenever the sad or glad feeling occurred, your physiology would immediately reflect an appropriate reinforcing expression. Let's say that right now I feel good. To feel bad, all I would have to do is reverse the cause-effect process and hold myself in the classic posture of a person who feels bad for a few minutes. What would happen? In a few minutes I would be wondering why I feel so blue. On the other hand, if right now I am emotionally flat, or even sad, if I adopted the posture and physiological expressions of someone who was happy and energized, in a few minutes the veil of sadness would lift. I would be feeling good. Try it out.

What does this mean to you? It means that if you want to feel good all the time, hold your body and present yourself *physiologically* as someone who does feel good. And you know what? You will feel good. And what's more, you will have an energizing effect on everybody you encounter. Think of the flip side, when you have had to look at someone who was depressed and blue, and purveyed an aura of gloom and doom. What happened to your energy level? It started to decline. Imagine being a buyer and having to look at a Willy Loman, who drags himself into your office, sinks into a chair opposite, exudes the misery of the day, and says, in effect, "You don't want to buy anything, do you?" Guaranteed, it will be a short interview.

Feelings, Action, and Achieving

When it comes to feeling good, simply act enthusiastic, hold the physiology of a person who feels good, and voila, you will feel good. When you feel good, you put yourself into an achieving state. What is an achieving state? This is the internal disposition to act, to do something, to move ahead, to accomplish, to achieve. Bundled with it is the desire, the want, the felt need to be satisfied. Without it nothing happens—no action, no forward movement, no wise use of time. With it, all things are possible because it disposes a person to move into action. *Nothing* ever gets done without action. This is why putting yourself into an achieving state is so important.

But an important question arises: Can we get into an achieving state only by first feeling good? No; sometimes feeling bad, or pain in its myriad expressions, propels a person into action. But even then, it is the desire to avoid continuing the pain or the wish to feel better that is the driving force to do something about one's problem. Nevertheless, the importance of enthusiasm, and feeling good, is that it makes getting into an achieving state so much easier. The easier something is, the more likely it is that someone will do it.

Regardless of the propelling force, good feelings or pain, when you are in an achieving state, you are ready to *do* something, and when you hook up this motive power with goals you want, the steps to take will present themselves in short order. So good feelings are the fuel; turning the key in the ignition occurs when you act, when you act you overcome inaction or inertia, and the forward momentum carries with it its own propensity to continue. It is important to understand this power of momentum, but in order to reap its reinforcing energy, it is necessary to do what? *Begin!* In physics, more power is needed to overcome inertia than to keep something moving. This is also true in life, in achieving goals, in feeling good. Just start. Where? Anywhere! Once you start, you're in motion, and it is easier to correct a wrong path than to start an entirely new one. So start anywhere. To summarize the flow, it looks like this: good feelings (or desire for same)—achieving state—beginning—forward momentum—correction—more purposeful action—achievement of goals.

Since getting into an achieving state is the key to achieving, to great sales and a great life, what else can you do to get into it?

Anchoring

Anchoring is a term used to describe a process that identifies a trigger that brings on a certain feeling. For example, for many Olympic gold-medal athletes, standing on the pedestal and hearing their national anthem induces a full spectrum of feelings ranging from pride to patriotism, gratitude, and vindication, and many are brought to tears. Mothers, when they look at the face of their baby, get filled with joy. Dog owners, when they come through the door and Fido wags his tail, smile with happiness. Or remember some smells from your childhood. To this day, when I smell gasoline, I feel happy because when I was a little boy, every year my father would take our family to the seashore for the summer. Before we left the city, we would always stop to fill up the gas tank. So the smell of gasoline got associated with excitement, anticipation, and fun for me. People can get anchored by sights, sounds, smells, touches, tastes. When they experience an anchor, it brings on the complex of feelings that they had previously associated with it. In other words, they were conditioned to reexperience the feelings associated with the earlier experiences when they were exposed to the anchor.

For example, when Ivan Pavlov, a noted scientist, showed a dog a piece of meat, the dog would salivate. When the dog salivated, Pavlov rang a bell. He repeated the process of showing the dog the meat, the dog salivating, and ringing the bell over and over. At a given point, all Pavlov had to do was to ring the bell and the dog would salivate. At that point he would say that the dog was conditioned to salivate on the ring of the bell. Likewise, we have been conditioned by so many things in our lives it is incredible. When some folks have to meet an authority figure, they approach the encounter in fear and trembling because when they were little, they had some bad experiences with authority figures that engendered those emotions. Some others, when asked to speak in public, dissolve in fear and panic because in the past when they had occasion to speak in public, they did a pitiful job. The speaking environment is the anchor that triggers these feelings. On the other hand, when some men smell the leather in a baseball glove, they almost burst with good feelings because it triggers the good feelings of youth.

This process of anchoring, or conditioning, can be done with premeditation and used to put you into an achieving state, the state that is the prelude to dynamic action. Here are the steps:

1. Think of a time when you accomplished something, and you were thrilled at having done so.
2. In your mind's eye, get in touch with the scene and the feelings, and let them bubble up to the surface of your awareness; then smile as you behold this internal experience.
3. While you're experiencing these feelings, tighten both fists and, holding your arms at your side at a 90-degree angle, say loudly, and with vigor, yes!
4. Repeat this same process five more times—the picture, the feelings, the fists, and yes!

What you have just done is to anchor your feelings of enthusiasm to the external gesture of fists and the word yes. In the future, just as Pavlov could make the dog salivate by simply ringing the bell, all you have to do to bring on the feelings associated with your accomplishment is to make the fists and say yes! with vigor and conviction.

If after testing it out you don't get suffused with those earlier feelings, repeat the process another five times, making the picture more vivid and the feelings more intense. This should do it. If not, come back tomorrow and do it again.

So, if you are about to go in and see a prospect, and you want to present yourself with an aliveness that flows from the inside, before you get out of your car, make the fists and say yes! with energy, and you will immediately put yourself in an achieving state. Test it out. I do it every time before I speak in front of an audience, and I know it helps me present myself in a positive, energetic manner.

A Homing Thought

Another simple technique that can help you change your feelings into a good feeling state is to focus on a homing thought. This is a thought that you like to come back to that has positive feelings associated with it, e.g., thinking of your baby, a placid scene of your own creation, your beloved, your garden, your pet, or a trip you want to take. Choose one, and at interludes during the day, reflect on it and see how it makes you feel. Those good feelings are once again putting you into an achieving state.

Momentum—for Good or Ill

Think of the times in the past when you have either been in a neutral state, unproductive, avoiding work, caught up in a bad habit, or downright depressed—in other words, in a nonachieving state. Think about the actions you engaged in that led to that feeling state. Make it specific. How did it begin? What action started the momentum, how did the momentum become imperious, how did it lead to further actions that made you feel guilty, and how did you feel the rest of the day?

Momentum can work for you or against you. Take, for example, a man who wants to stop smoking cigarettes. He realizes it is a bad habit, but somehow the devil gets him, or so he would lead you to believe. What happens is that the thought is father to the act. The thought of a smoke flits across his consciousness; it is held on to; a pack of cigarettes is actually seen, and then purchased. By then the snowball is hurtling down the hill. Momentum takes over, and the habit gets repeated and repeated. Each time it's repeated, it gets reinforced. What do we have here? Another case of conditioning. The addict is anchored into the image of a pack of butts,

and once it's entertained, momentum kicks in, and all the supporting actions flow effortlessly from that point in time.

These anchors set a person up for good or ill—e.g., for an alco-
holic, drinking behavior is anchored in the image of the drink; for
a sex addict, behavior is anchored in the image of the breast, leg,
or buns; for an actor, in the smell of greasepaint; for a sugar addict,
in the sight of a chocolate bar. The image can be either a thought
pictured and entertained in the mind, or the sight of an object in
real life. Either can trigger the unfolding behavior.

To gain control of your life, your feelings, your time, your behavior, two things are necessary: (1) identify the positive anchors
in your experience that put you into an achieving state, and use
them repeatedly as needed, and (2) identify and avoid the anchors
that historically have led you into a nonachieving state. How? Simply by not giving them air time, by not reflecting on them, by not
holding them in your imagination or consciousness for any time at
all. And when they do slip into your consciousness, interrupt the
momentum by focusing on a positive anchor or a homing thought,
or by changing your physiology—go for a walk, focus on your
breathing, snap a rubber band against your wrist, sing a song, re-
cite a poem, run, jog, or associate the thought with some disgusting
image. Any of these will help move you toward an achieving state.

Summary and Bridge

Feelings ripple through virtually everything that we experience
and vary in their degree of intensity. Feelings can be a cause and
an effect. In Chapters 1 and 2 I have shown you how to use enthusiasm and other positive feelings to put you into an achieving state.
Once you understand the incredible power of feelings, you can use
them to your advantage. Any of the techniques mentioned, when
utilized on a regular basis, can help you to feel good all the time,
i.e., physiology, anchoring, a homing thought, and momentum.
When you live life applying these techniques, not only will you
enjoy the trip, but you will be disposed to do great things in sales
and in life.

In subsequent chapters I will show you how some of the other
rings profoundly affect your feelings, and how you can utilize your

choices, your beliefs, and your relationships to enhance your good feelings and, by extension, put you and keep you, all the more, in an achieving state. In the next chapter, the quintessential sale that you need to make will provide you with a solid ground for pervasive good feelings.

3

The Quintessential Sale

	Yes	No
1. Would you like to discover the one thing that can make you free?	☐	☐
2. Would you like to unleash the power in you that is the ground for all your experiences?	☐	☐
3. Would you like to be in touch with the springboard to greatness in sales *and* greatness in life?	☐	☐

The single most important sale you can make is to sell *yourself on yourself.* Why? If you don't, you will always have that ache inside, even if your sales numbers break through the roof. Remember, the goal of this book is to help you not only to get great sales, but to have a great life. A great life is a happy life. It is kind of pointless, in my judgment, to be a high-achieving star salesperson, and at the same time be a miserable wretch. When this is chronic, a person truly misses the trip.

In order to make this quintessential sale, I want you to do an

exercise with me, and follow my reasoning carefully while applying it to yourself every step along the way. Below is a scale from 0
to 10. On the left is the word *self-worth*, and on the right is *role*. By
self-worth I mean how you feel about yourself, your sense of
worth, your sense of value. It is a judgment about you, your identity. By role I mean the different hats that you wear, e.g., father,
mother, manager, salesperson, golfer, church member, citizen. At
any given time, you tend to be operating in one role or another.

Focus, if you will, on the self-worth side of the scale, and on
that scale from 0 to 10, make some estimate of how you feel about
yourself. Zero is a complete and utter disaster, and 10 is that than
which there is no higher. Make that judgment and jot that number
down. Now move to the role side of the scale. In your mind's eye,
pick out one role that is important to you. It could be your occupational role, e.g., salesperson, or a family role like husband, wife,
son, or daughter. Do you have that role in your mind? Yes? Now
make some estimate of how you perform in that role. Zero is a
complete wipe-out, and 10 is crest of the hill. Jot that number
down.

Self-Worth	Role
-10-	
-9-	
-8-	
-7-	
-6-	
-5-	
-4-	
-3-	
-2-	
-1-	
-0-	

Here is what I have discovered: There is a complete integration
between how a person feels about himself or herself in terms of the

sense of self-worth and how that person performs in roles that are important to him or her. For example, suppose I asked a young man, "What did you give yourself in terms of your self-worth?" and he said, "I gave myself a 5." Then I said, "What role did you choose that was important to you?" Suppose he replied, "I chose my occupational role, salesman—that sure is important to me." Then I asked him what score he gave himself in terms of his performance in that role. Very likely that young man would say that his performance came in somewhere between 4 and 6. Now reflect on your two scores and see if your role score is within one number, up or down, from your self-worth score. I have asked that question of over five thousand people, and typically 90 percent or more affirm that their role score is within one point, up or down, of their self-worth score. If I asked that young man if he knew how to be a 10 as a salesman, he would in all probability say, "Sure, I know how to be a 10 as a salesman. I know how to prospect, make appointments, interview prospects, find out if they have any interest and any money to spend, find out who would make the decision, handle objections, close, get referrals, organize my day, and operate according to priorities. I also know where to find books, tapes, and seminars on how to be a great salesman. In other words, I know how to be a 10 as a salesman." But what I have observed is that most people, in the roles that are important to them, tend to operate at a level half of what they already know how to! Why? It's not because there is anything mysterious or esoteric about what you would have to do to be a 10 as a salesperson—that knowledge is out there, available, and not too difficult to master. The same is true whether you're dealing with law, parenting, nursing, painting, or whatever. The real reason—or a core reason—why most people operate the way they do is over in the self-worth column. People operate consistent with their sense of self-worth. Their performance range is their comfort zone, and that is dictated by their level of self-worth. (See the young salesman above with a 5 in self-worth, and a 4 to 6 in actual performance as a salesman.)

Now, what do you think would happen if that young man, in terms of his *self-worth*, made himself a 10? How would it affect his performance as a salesman? It would put him into the 9 to 10 category in terms of performance. Why? Because of the consistency between a person's self-worth and that person's performance in roles that are important to him or her. There is an innate drive to hit our comfort zone, and the comfort zone flows out of self-worth.

Now, reflect on what you gave yourself in terms of your self-worth. Most folks, when asked that question, usually reply that they gave themselves less than a 10. Most of those who do give themselves a 10 do so for the wrong reason. When asked why they gave themselves less than a 10, they answer that it would be conceited, boastful, or not possible because a 10 represented perfection, or because they have done some or many bad or inept things in their life.

Well, let me tell you what I believe you are, and I will do everything I can to persuade you that it is the case. When it comes to your self-worth, you are a 10.

You are born into the world as a 10, but unfortunately, for many, from that first little swat on the behind it is steadily downhill. Think of those children living in a household where day in and day out they are hearing messages of this order: "What's the matter with you? Can't you do anything right? You are a total disaster. You're a bad boy! I can't trust you as far as I can throw you! You're always screwing up! Some day you're going to wind up behind bars! Can't you be like your sister? What will your grandmother think when she hears what you did? Or your teachers? You disgust me! I'm fed up with you!"

The child starts out as a 10, but in no time, what do you think parents have on their hands? A frog! And how do you think a frog behaves? Exactly as you suspected—the child underachieves; is disruptive, destructive, vandalistic, or violent; or possibly withdraws, becomes a Nintendo freak, or is inhibited and surly. And how does the child feel? Inferior, angry, sad, and filled with misery and pain. The child finds a way to prove to Mom and Pop that they are right. That's where the program gets set. But all is not lost; if that was the rock you were put under, you can climb out from under it—if you really want to.

I have asserted, "You are a 10." Let me tell you why I see you as a 10, and I would suggest that what I am about to say is not a throwaway belief. In my judgment, it is the rock-bottom foundation for happiness, for peace of mind. It is a springboard to excellence in sales or whatever performance arena is important to you, and it is one of the greatest insulators against the stress and adver-

sity of life that I know of. What's more, this judgment about yourself is the perspective through which you experience life on this
planet. Everything you do, say, feel, see, touch, hear, taste, or sense
is filtered through your self-worth judgment, and depending on
what that judgment about yourself is, it will either be a ball and
chain or a truly liberating belief.

You are a 10 because you are a person of worth, of dignity, of
value. You are important; you are beautiful; you are precious; you
are priceless—we could not put a dollar value on you. You are
interesting; you are a good person; you have the seeds of greatness
inside of you, and this is not hyperbole! You are special. Not only
are you special, you have a special destiny, and by some strange
coincidence your special destiny and my special destiny have
crossed—as you are reading these very words—and I am excited
about that! And one last thing: Nothing is wrong with you, and
nothing was ever wrong with you! That's why you are a 10. Now
please, read this last paragraph over again and again, slowly letting these concepts inside of you because they can have profound
consequences to you as you create your special destiny.

The Bill of Goods Most of Us Have Been Sold

Most of us have been taught, from the time we were little boys
and girls to the present moment, what really constitutes a person's
worth and value. Following is a long list of the measures people
(society) use to judge your worth and value: money, beauty, occupation, educational level, where you live, the kind of house you
live in, ethnic/racial background, gender, age, accent of language,
marital status, sexual preference, where you vacation, possessions
(e.g., car, labels in your clothes, jewelry, the make of your watch,
the kind of stereo), and so forth. And when you are young, for a
boy, athletic ability; and for a girl, attractiveness. The rules are simple: If you have these things, you are somebody; if you don't, you
are nobody.

Who teaches us these things? Our parents, our extended family, television, peers, magazines, movies. The messages are unrelenting and pervasive; everywhere you look, you can see the kind
of people who are revered, respected, and paid attention to. Ma-

donna's "Material Girl" really captures the measures so many embrace.

Don't get me wrong. There is nothing wrong with any of these attributes, achievements, or possessions. In themselves they are good. That's not the point. The point is that in order to be a 10, you don't *need* any of this stuff. And the paradox is that when you really realize you don't need it, apart from certain ascribed characteristics like gender, color, and height, you can have as much as you want and are willing to go after. But you don't need it to be somebody—you already are somebody!

The problem is that when you believe that you need some or many of the indicators of worth and value listed above, when you don't have them, you worry about getting them, and when you get them, you worry about losing them. If you have them and then lose them, what happens to your worth and value? It goes right down the drain. For many who have invested themselves in these perceptions, this is devastating, and it is very difficult to bounce back. In fact, if you want to live in a very fragile world, all you have to do is to believe the bill of goods; you will have stress at every turn of the screw—guaranteed. Everywhere you turn, you will have an opportunity to feel inferior. Why? Because there is always someone richer, healthier, prettier, more fit, or with some new toy that is bigger or better than yours. Other realities also set in: We grow old, get sick, lose our hair, get fired, lose money, fail, get rejected, get divorced, get shelved, get cut, or (the worst bummer of all) die. These phenomena are ineluctable, and face lifts, hair transplants, and personal trainers only slow the irreversible temporarily. If you believe you *need* any of these things to be okay, you have a basic design for self-imposed misery.

The further fact is that there is no one on this planet better than you (and, of course, there is no one who is worse than you, but it is the former, with the pervasive feelings of inferiority, that plagues so many people).

Some folks, when they have accumulated many of the indicators of success above, take comfort that they have made it, and feel better than those who have not. But if their son or daughter, for example, refuses to adhere to their lifestyle choices, like marrying the "right" kind of person or going to the "right" school, often bitter warfare occurs. So often the possession or lack of these attri-

butes or things is the subject of scheming, comparisons and manip-
ulations, which serve to destroy love in a relationship.

But what do I want to shout from a mountain top? You don't
have to compare yourself to anybody. You already are somebody.
You are special. You are a 10.

Why Is It Important?

Let me compare it to a person who feels like a 2 in terms of his or
her sense of self-worth. Psychologists tell us that in the first five to
seven years of life, everybody makes a life position decision about
himself or herself. And although it can have a hundred thousand
nuances, the 2s make a moral judgment about themselves. A 2
makes the judgment, "I am bad." How do they come to this conclusion? The significant big people in their lives have told them, by
word, deed, and omission, that they are bad, they are dumb, they
are not as good as . . . , they have done *that* unforgivable thing.
Little people, having a very narrow scope of experience, accept
these definitions as true, and emotionalize them to such an extent
that in extreme cases they can go to the grave with this searing
pain inside of them.

In most households, when a little boy or little girl is bad, what
happens? He or she gets punished; he or she gets spanked. In fact,
as that person grows up, unless something really neat has happened to that person, you could, for example, wind up with a
forty-two-year-old man who, despite the accouterments of success,
inside feels low-down and miserable. Without articulating it, he
knows that he deserves to be punished. And if you take a look at
his behavior as his life unravels, it looks as if he is saying, "I have
to find a way to be miserable." And of course, what do you think
happens? You talk about creativity. There is no limit to the creative
imagination when it comes to finding ways to be miserable. And
the 2s do succeed.

Although 2s come in a myriad of types, let me describe some
things you will find when you encounter many of them. First of
all, look at their faces. Faces are the road maps to feelings, and you
can't hide feelings. These people often have that hangdog look of
sadness and frown a lot. Some look like frightened rabbits, with

fear being one of their fundamental experiences. They are not into taking any risks. Why? Because if they take a risk and fail, they then go public with something they know to be true privately, namely, that they are 2s, schmucks, schlemiels, losers, jerks, nerds, has-beens, failures. In order *not* to use a megaphone to announce their own belief about their self-worth to everybody, they simply do not take any risks. And what happens? Not much, because if you, or anyone, do not take risks, you do not grow. So look at their lives: They never venture far from home base or do anything exciting, they make few contributions, and even if they are Michelangelos, they never take their creative expressions out of the closet.

What if the 2 is a salesperson? Well, there are many paths that he or she can go down, but here are a number of common ones. First of all, he or she is part of the cohort of sales novices that don't make it, because as anyone who has ever done sales knows, initially, selling is not easy. There is a painful learning curve, with a lot of mistakes, failures, and rejections. Many 2s can't bear the pain, and, as a consequence, once they have sold their product to their friends and relatives, they flee the profession. Those who stay operate in a variety of ways. One type finds their comfort zone at a level consistent with 2ness. They are on the bottom tail of the performance curve, and many have a hard time even achieving that. If they are outside salespeople, you will often find them escaping to the movies in the afternoon, or the golf course, or a bar. Others call on friends or old customers or spend prime selling time in the office. On the other hand, you can have a hard-driving, high-achieving salesperson who breaks all records, wins all the contests, but inside is fundamentally a frightened child. Many a sales manager might say, "Give me all the high-achieving not-OK salespeople you can find—that's just fine with me." The problem with this type of individual is that there are always hidden costs. They may not get expressed in customer relations, but this discrepancy between feelings of self-worth and high performance means internal stress, pain, unhappiness, and misery—that acid ball of discontent. Often these folks get into painkillers like alcohol, smoking, drugs, or sex, or unload their pain in destructive abuse of their spouse and children. Words like peace, serenity, joy, happiness, fulfillment, and intimacy are not even in their vocabulary, and if perchance they do indeed experience any of these, it is invariably

fleeting. Where is their ball and chain? It is not in technique or
the ability to hit their numbers, it is on the self-worth side of the
equation.

What also happens is that these 2s often define themselves as
victims when adversity strikes. Nothing is ever their fault. It's always somebody else's fault. If they lose a sale or their sales numbers dip, it's their dumbbell customer's fault, or the economy, the
weather, the time of month, the high price management has set on
their product, the factory, shipping, the inadequacy of the advertis-
ing, or whatever. So what do they do with their time and energy?
They sit around moaning, groaning, complaining, blaming, and
(worst) waiting. They wait for the solution of their sales problem,
or virtually any other problem, to come from outside of themselves. And my rule of thumb is that anyone who sits around and
waits for good things to happen is holding a losing hand. Good
things rarely happen to those who are waiting.

If you examine the language of these 2s, you will hear their
favorite words, over and over: "I can't" or, even more definitively,
"no." Any new idea thrown on the table is greeted with "We can't
do that," "It has never been done before," or "It won't work."
They are the negatives, the naysayers, the dream killers, and they
kill not only their own dreams, but everyone else's.

You will also find that characteristically, and routinely, these
2s, whether high or low achievers, engage in the single most destructive thing that can go on between two people, and that is *criticism*. Why? Because about 80 percent of the time, when criticism is
delivered, it is not done kindly, with an eye to helping the other
person grow, but just the opposite. It is intended to hurt, wipe out,
denigrate, checkmate, or punish the target of the criticism, or simply to offload some of the pain the 2 is feeling inside. What is the
consequence? Well, think about the times when you were on the
receiving end of criticism. How did it feel? I'll tell you. It hurt, it
irritated, it made you angry, and maybe it even filled you with
hateful feeling. What did you want to do? Flee, get out of there,
get away from that person, or strike back. That's what criticism
does. It distances people; it estranges people; it cools the relationship; and in many cases the people who are criticized will come
back with their own criticisms, or engage in superior firepower,
like violence or killing. In many cases criticism will kill the rela-

tionship. Often, for example, what precedes a divorce is a long history of verbal combat, with two former lovers hurtling criticisms at each other. Often when kids run away from home, or as adults don't communicate much with Mom or Pop, the reason is simply that Mom and Pop brought the child up in the Attila the Hun tradition of child rearing, with an ongoing tide of criticism, snide remarks, sarcasm, condemning judgments, corrections, or intolerant remarks. At some point the child often says, in effect, "I can't take it anymore" and bolts for the door, in many cases never to return.

There are many other ways in which 2s make themselves miserable. For example, when they have a problem, they spend their time exclaiming, "Why did this have to happen to me?" "Why me?" This is an endless loop question. They ask such questions over and over again, and what is the effect? It cements them deeper and deeper into their victimization, their powerlessness. It's a classic go-nowhere, "dog chasing tail" posture.

Some, in their quest to be miserable, get fixated on the past, and exhibit a disease called "if onlyitis." All they have to do to bring on their favorite bad feeling is to plug in the videotape in their head and run the "if onlys." "If only I had taken that job with Honeywell." "If only the boss liked me." "If only I were a man." "If only I hadn't married that meatball." "If only I had a degree." What's the payoff? Bad feelings and a disposition that puts the person in a nonachieving state.

Other 2s get hung up on the future and exhibit another disease called "what ifitis." "What if I don't hit my numbers?" "What if I don't get this order?" "What if I get passed over for promotion?" "What if I my company downsizes and I am out of a job?" "What if I get cancer of the breast?" They spend all their time worrying about impending catastrophes, 99.9 percent of which never happen. Typically they experience a case of galloping anxiety. The heart beats faster and faster, and often the rate becomes elevated permanently; they develop high blood pressure and become candidates for heart attack, stroke, and atherosclerosis, and, in many cases, an early demise.

There is another class of people who are so versatile in making themselves miserable that they go back and forth between the past and the future, between the "what ifs" and the "if onlys," so that they are rarely on this planet. What happens to them? In effect, they miss the trip because all that you and I have in the final analysis is the *now*. If at any given now a person is off in the blue rehearsing the miseries of yesterday or worrying about the catastrophes of tomorrow, he or she is not in the now. The now is where life is, where love is, where affection is given and received, where creativity is, where involvement is, and where enriching experiences occur. Such a blue-skyer winds up with no enriching experiences, no memories, no stories to tell, and after he is gone, about all the folks standing around his tombstone can think of to have chiseled on it is, "He breathed."

Again, in summary, what is the consequence of this 2ness for one in sales? The probability is that it will lead in most cases to inadequate performance, and most definitely to heavy-duty pain, regardless of performance level. The effects raise a very fundamental existential question: Why am I on this planet? You have two choices, to be happy or to be miserable. If misery is your present experience and happiness makes sense, then please read on—even if you are not now miserable.

The Importance of Seeing Yourself as a 10

My task here is not to teach you how to be miserable (most people don't tend to need lessons on that), but rather to point out what can happen to people when they indeed know that they are 10s and what profound consequences such a belief can have for star performance as a salesperson, and for building a great life.

As I pointed out earlier, psychologists say that we make a life position decision about ourselves in that five- to seven-year period. The 10s have made one, and it too is a moral judgment. Its expression can take many forms, but it comes down to, "I am a *good* person." How do they come to this conclusion? The significant big people in their lives told them so; they dandled them on their knee, cherished them, cared for them, loved them in word and deed. Basically, they persuaded these little people that they were indeed 10s. Now, in most households, when a little boy or girl behaves properly, what does he or she get? He or she gets rewarded. So if you look at how the lives of 10s unfold over time, they look, although they may never consciously articulate it, as if they know that they deserve to be happy, and it looks as if their behavior is saying, "I will find a way to be happy." And what happens to the 10s? They find a way. I am not saying that they do not experience tragedy, disappointment, sadness, setbacks, or problems; what I am saying is that when they do experience these adversities in life, they do not make a career out of it. For example, when 2s fail at something, they quickly follow it up with a condemning judgment—"I am a failure." When 10s fail at something, they get back to the drawing board real fast and ask themselves questions like "What can I do about it?" "What can I learn from this failing experience?" "How have others solved this problem?" In fact, the 10s are not afraid to take a risk, because the worst thing that can happen is that they might learn something from the experience. What this posture does is to embolden the 10s to take risks, and they do. Not rash risks, like betting the farm on a roll of the dice, but reasonable ones that stretch them into the unknown, where they learn new skills, test out ideas and plans, and venture into places they have never been before, whether geographically, intellectually, or spiritually. And what is the payoff? They grow, and come closer and closer to their full potential as human beings. The 10s get turned on by life, by the possibilities for fun, joy, adventure, contribution, service. They are not victims of circumstance, but creators of opportunity; they are not waiting for good things to happen, they *make* good things happen, knowing that there is no Santa Claus or fairy godmother who is going to plunk it all down on their doorstep. They have a bias for action, knowing that nothing happens without it. They are active and proactive, looking and anticipating, and creating ways to enrich their own lives and the lives of others.

What kind of feelings do the 10s have? The full gamut of human emotion, but they know intuitively that it makes more sense to feel good most of the time, and after the natural experience of feelings like sadness, anger, or loss, they move swiftly into a feel-good state, start solving their problems, and get on with it. When someone throws a new idea on the table, they respond by saying, "What's good about it?" or "Let's test it out." They are into possibilities, problem solving, exploring, testing, tweaking, and improving. Further, they know that good things don't happen by chance, so they are goal setters; they have plans, and they take steps to make them happen.

But the 10s know something else. They know that it is not enough to sit around their room all day hugging themselves, saying "I'm a 10; I'm a 10; I'm a 10," and thinking that they have it all wrapped up. They know that one of the great opportunities they have is that they can help others feel like 10s. How do they do that? There are a thousand ways to show other people that they are special, that they are important, that you care for them, but the one way that is the most powerful is to give the other people air time—to listen to their story. The incredible thing about being a listener is that when you do listen, the other person feels valued, feels good, feels like a 10. The enlightened 10s bring listening to a high art, and the payoff is that they are never lonely, because they have found the one thing that can make them uncommon people on this planet, and that is listening to others. This profound skill will be elaborated upon later.

The 10s know another thing: that they are special and that they have a special destiny. They are in the process of writing out their autobiography, just as you are. You have the pen in your hand. Chapters 1, 2, and 3 were written by mother and father; 4, 5, and 6 by your teachers, preachers, and the mass media; but wherever you are in your life story, you can decide what you want to put in the next chapter or chapters. And when others pick up your life story, do you want them to fall asleep reading Chapter 8 or get a migraine reading the accounts of all your problems? Do you want them to close the book saying, "She was a brick" or, "Is that it?" or, "What a waste!" or do you want them to say, "Wow, what a life!" or, "Fantastic!" or, "Where is Part II?"

Each of us has two tools that are going to get us through our life path; one is our body, and the other is our mind. The 10s know this, and, as a consequence, they are committed to optimum good health. They are conscious of what they do to their body, what they eat, what they drink, how they exercise, and how they can stay fit. You will not find amongst the 10s the two-pack-a-day smokers, or the alcoholics, or the obese. Why? Because they are so conscious of their most valuable irreversible resource—time—that they are doing everything they can to maximize the chances of creating a special destiny that is long and full, to their genetic limit.

Further, when they graduated from school, they didn't take their brain and put it into formaldehyde. They make living a life-long learning proposition. They read, they study, they listen, they experience. They become masters of their craft, whether it is selling or fathering or mothering, and they are always trying to discover a better way.

The incredible thing about this whole discussion of your 10ness is that if perchance you were brought up in a snake pit and concluded that you were not a 10, the one thing that you (and I) can do (and this is *the* unique human power) is to choose to see yourself in a life-enhancing manner, as a 10. How to make that election, and get it in deep, is what the next chapter is all about.

In conclusion, I would like you to see yourself as a 10, feel like a 10, believe you are a 10. And when you do, you will have discovered the big ripple that can support all your efforts to be great in sales *and* in life!

Summary and Bridge

Affirming your worth and value as a person is the lever to achieve liberation. Once you see that you are not what you do or what you have, and that your basic worth does not depend on labels, cars, swimming pools, degrees, achievement, beauty, or gender, but that you already are somebody, you will be giving yourself a yes! It is the quintessential sale, the quintessential yes! that can truly transport you to greatness.

The next chapter will spell out some ways you can get these concepts in deep, so that they become a habitual posture in which you experience life.

4

How to Get It in Deep

	Yes	No
1. Would you like to have your 10ness send up ripples that permeate every area of your life?	☐	☐
2. Would you like to experience the world every single day from a perspective of freedom?	☐	☐
3. Would you like to know how to close on yourself again and again?	☐	☐

It's great to know you are a 10, choose it, accept it, and believe it. It's a start to having positive ripples touch every area of your life in profound ways. But how do you get it in deep? How can you approach the world habitually from the perspective of your 10ness? How can you have it transform your view of yourself and your relations with others, unleash your creativity, enhance your problem-solving ability, make your performance as a salesperson go off the charts? How can you get it to help you carve out a special destiny that you are truly proud of?

I suggest you take the ten steps to 10ness, read them every day for the next thirty days, and do what they instruct. In no time people will be coming up to you and saying, "You know, there is something different about you. I can't put my finger on it, but you seem different. You carry yourself differently; you look different." They will be seeing your 10ness in action. They simply won't have the words to articulate what is different, except that you are different, and it's better!

Try these steps to get it in deep, so you can maximize the ripple effect.

1. *The unique human power is the power to choose. Choose to see yourself in a life-enhancing manner.* Choose to see yourself as a 10. Choose to experience life from now on as a 10. But this choice is not just made once. Make the choice every day. It is the choice that is the gateway to a quality life, one filled with enriching experiences, much love, and intimacy. Your world begins and ends inside of you, and everything that comes in is filtered through this judgment about yourself. It is the fundamental support for a positive attitude and a perspective of hope in a context of optimism.

How do you make the choice? Simply say, softly but with feeling and passion, "I choose to see myself as a 10." Each day, say it, feel it, and believe it. That choice will get cemented into your self view, and the self-worth judgment will be a liberating one.

2. *To get your choice in deep, repeat over and over, fifty times a day, statements like the following:* "I am a 10; I am special; I have a special destiny; I have all I need to create a quality life. I am making it happen." Put these affirmations on a 3-by-5-inch card, and carry it around with you. Anytime there is a lull or waiting time, or before or after dealing with a client, read it and feel it. Let this be your mantra.

Repetition is the mother and father of learning. In the past, the way you developed a habit, whether good or bad, was by repeating acts over and over again until they got programmed into your neural pathways so deeply that you didn't even have to think about them. Remember the first time you got behind the wheel of a car and tried to steer, accelerate, shift, observe signs, and watch out for pedestrians and cars in the other lane. You wondered how anybody could do it. But you came out the second time, and the third time, and by the fourth time, you could steer, shift, drive, and even chew gum all at the same time. By the fifth time, you could steer, shift, chew gum, and even hold a conversation. Today you don't think about any of these steps because driving skill has become a habit. What I am talking about here is developing a habit of thinking about yourself. The key to developing a habitual perspective about yourself is repetition. By repeating the affirmation of your 10ness over and over and over, after a while something incredible occurs: you come to believe it. Once you believe it, making it a stronger and deeper belief so that it becomes a habitual way of experiencing life is the goal.

3. Another way to get this belief about yourself in deep is to *tap your creative imagination and, in particular, the movie-making capability that you and I have.* Each day, in a quiet time, with eyes closed, see yourself in bright living color going through the day acting like a 10, feeling thrilled about it, and projecting your 10ness to others in your life. See yourself relating to your spouse and children knowing that you are a 10. See yourself calling on a client, and get a sense of how it feels to know that you are indeed a 10. In your mind's eye, see yourself walking like a 10, talking like a 10, working like a 10, playing like a 10. While you're seeing it, smile, once again say yes! and let the feelings of 10ness permeate every cell in your body and mind.

You can do this simple exercise in as little time as one minute, or you can get into it and let it go on as long as you are comfortable. What you are doing in your imagination is a type of mental rehearsal. You are practicing in your mind. The most knowledgeable coaches in sports all know the power of having the appropriate mental images. They tell their charges to see the act as completed in their mind. Many athletes at the frontier of sports training see the act in their mind before they do it. When, just before his event in the Montreal Olympics in 1976, Howard Cosell asked Edwin Moses, a high hurdler, how he felt about his chances, Moses said, "Howard, I can taste it." He meant that he was going to win: he could feel it, see it, and taste the cup of victory.

So what am I saying here? See yourself as a 10 in your mind. And what will happen in your mind will become your reality. The pictures in your mind will reinforce your belief, and the belief, energized by feelings while you are in a quiet time with your eyes closed, will deepen the program. Done regularly, it will become a habit.

4. *Put up visual reminders of your 10ness, and that special destiny to which you are called.* The reason so many good people get distracted or unfocused, or let high-priority things wind up on the bottom of their "to do" list, is simply because they forget. What they need is reminders. If your 10ness is important to you, then put up symbolic reminders of it around your house, in your car, in your office, in your wallet, etc. Don't tell anyone else what they mean. Only you have to know. It could be something as simple as the number 10. This carries with it all the other connotations about your being special, capable, precious, interesting, important, good, worthwhile, of value, beautiful, and someone who is busy performing at a level consistent with your 10ness—someone who is creating a special destiny.

5. *Stop making self-condemning judgments about yourself.* Self-talk that sounds something like the following should be given zero air time: "I'm not so neat. I'm just ordinary. I can't do anything right. I always screw up. Other people are better, smarter, prettier, more talented, more capable, more attractive, richer, luckier, healthier, etc." You don't have to compare yourself to anyone, and invidious comparisons like these have only one consequence—they make you low-down, depressed, and miserable. Those invidious comparisons and negative judgments are part of the nonsense you were taught to believe about yourself in the first instance. Let them go.

What do you replace them with? Replace them with the affirmations on your 3- by 5-inch card. Replace them with the truth about yourself, your worth, your value, your incredible potential—and focus on those kinds of life-enhancing thoughts.

6. *Adopt the physiology of a 10.* Walk like a 10—head up, body erect, and moving briskly. Sit like a 10—up straight, with attention. Talk like a 10—inject your words with the power and feeling of enthusiasm. Put a smile on your face, and project your 10ness by the way you present yourself. And take care of your body; in fact, this is so important that I have devoted Chapter 7 to guidance on how to do it. Your physiology sends reinforcing and supporting

messages to your brain. Allowing belief in your 10ness to permeate your body as indicated tells the brain to flood your body with biochemicals that will raise your energy level and give you a high. Only this time you will be high on yourself for the right reasons.

7. *Model 10ness for those around you.* By letting your 10ness ripple through every aspect of your life and your relations with others, you make yourself an incredible model for others to imitate—your children, your spouse, your coworkers, your friends, and even your customers. Since most people out there are filled with varying degrees of pain, and happiness seems to be a fleeting experience for them, showing others how to be a free spirit who is turned on by life, possibility, adventure, fun, and service gives them an example to follow. They may never ask. It doesn't matter. You will leave your mark on others anyway. The mark, the impress, the impact, the effect of a 10 on others will always be a positive one.

8. *Seek out opportunities to help others feel like 10s.* This is so important that I have dedicated an entire chapter to it also, but this is the fact: The way most people operate is consistent with the reverse of the Golden Rule; "They do unto others as they do unto themselves." Most people do not see themselves as 10s. Most people have not accepted themselves, nor do they see the beauty inside of themselves. What they see is the ugliness, the dark side of themselves, the negative and hateful side of themselves. And what do they do to themselves? They engage nonstop in unrelenting self-criticism. That is bad enough, but note the reverse of the Golden Rule. That's what they do to others—criticize, criticize, criticize. In fact, they seek out opportunities to put others down and help them to feel like zeros. It is important to know that the folks who have a need to do this are speaking in code. They are really crying out for help and operating from fear. Under the negative condemning judgments and the attack is really a frightened little boy or girl. What can you do?

Once you know you are a 10, start acting like a 10, and start self-talking like a 10; then, like night follows day, that's what you tend to do to others. You are able to reach out in love to someone else; love, kindness, thoughtfulness, and caring flow out naturally. As a consequence of your reaching out and understanding the pain others have, most will feel like 10s in your presence. If they don't, it is because of their own static, not because of anything you are doing. When you are confronted with hostility, you will be an oasis of serenity, and you will understand the scam these unfortunates are playing on themselves.

9. *Anchor your 10ness in the same manner that you anchored enthusiasm.* This is called stacking the anchors. While you are holding an image of yourself acting and feeling like a 10, make fists of your hands, hold them at your side, and say yes! Repeat this with feeling at least five times. Now the feelings of enthusiasm that you anchored earlier will merge with your sense of 10ness, and you will have a powerful anchor that you can fire off whenever you want to heighten those feelings and get energized. The rippling effects of this act will become self-evident.

10. *Before you do anything, ask yourself, "Is this the highest and best use of my time?"* Your special destiny is yours to create. The 10s flee from mediocrity, and are committed to excellence in the things that are important to them. Excellence relates to the arena of performance behavior. Behavior takes place in time. Time is for doing—what? The things that are going to result in excellence, in a special destiny that is unique, in a biography that is amazing. So how do 10s feel about time? They revere it and acknowledge it as their most precious irreversible resource. The commitment to using it well is reinforced by asking yourself, when you are not on task or when you are wondering what it might make sense to do, "What is the highest and best thing for me to be doing right now?" Answering that question and making your behavior conform will be another of the millions of steps to take that will result in a great life.

Summary and Bridge

What do we have here? By following these guidelines, you will get your 10ness in deep, making it a habitual mindset through which you experience the world. Your sense of your self-worth will ripple through everything else you do. To reap the positive benefits of your fundamental source of energy—you, in your essence, in your identity—celebrate yourself by being a 10, and read this chapter periodically for reinforcement and inspiration.

In conclusion, choose to see yourself as a 10; repeat the affirmation of your 10ness over and over every day; visualize yourself
being and acting like a 10; put up visual reminders of your 10ness;
stop making invidious comparisons and self-condemning judgments about yourself; let go of the nonsense others and society
have taught you to believe about your self-worth; adopt the physiology of a 10; model 10ness for those you care about; help others
feel like 10s; ground your 10ness in your enthusiasm anchor; and
use time so well that creating each page of your autobiography is
an exemplar of the highest and best use of it.

The next chapter will deal with a method to fine-tune your
mind and your body. These are the instruments through which
you experience life. Knowing how to fine-tune them will support
your quintessential sale, your pursuit of goals, your energy, and
your basic happiness.

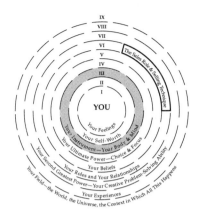

5

Mental Renewal

	Yes	No
1. Would you be interested in learning how to experience peace while seeing your creativity explode?	☐	☐
2. Is it important to you to be a high-energy person?	☐	☐
3. Are you looking for a simple but powerful way to cope with the stress of life?	☐	☐

Your life, your experiences, your feelings, your relationships with others all begin and end in your mind. Your mind is you; your mind is your source of meaning. Your mind will dictate how you feel, what you see, and how you react. Your mind is the emotional responsive and proactive core of your personal existence. To understand your mind, a couple of analogies might help.

When a violinist prepares to play a concerto, what is the first thing she does with her instrument? She tunes it. Imagine what would happen if she took the violin out of its case and simply proceeded to play the notes of the score in front of her. It would very probably be out of key, send a shrillness and atonality through the performance that would inflict pain on the audience, and hold the performance itself up to ridicule. It would not matter that the violinist's technique was exquisite, nor that the fingering, the faithfulness to the composer's notes, or the drama and subtlety that the artist extruded from the instrument was amazing. If the instrument was not tuned properly at the outset, the performance would clearly be subpar, and certainly not all that it could have been.

Think of your mind as your instrument. It has incredible potential to create amazing things, to experience life to its fullest, to make contributions that profoundly affect others, to feel great all the time, and to know love, peace, and serenity. In order to actualize this potential, it is necessary for you to tune your instrument every time you take it out of its case.

Before I spell out the implications of the preceding analogy, imagine that you are going on a one-thousand-mile trip to a mountain retreat. You decide to use your automobile. What are the things you do to your automobile to prepare it for the journey? You take it to a garage, get it tuned, change the oil, check all systems, and then, before you leave the station, fill up the tank. You go home fully confident that when you start the journey the next day, you will complete it successfully. Along the way to your destination, you will stop periodically to note your gas, your oil, and your water levels just to make sure everything is going fine. You will eventually reach your destination on time as planned.

On the other hand, what risks would you run if you undertook your journey without checking any of your car's systems? You could run out of gas, burn up your oilless engine, overheat because of a low coolant level, get a flat and have no spare, or snap an engine belt or your timing chain, to name just a few possible calamities. If any of these occurred, how would you feel? Stressed out and angry with yourself and whoever is with you. You would waste valuable time, get charged exorbitant fees for towing and repairs, and generally feel kind of sour about the entire ordeal.

Well, think of your life as a journey and every day as a leg of that journey. If you just let things happen, not much of great good does. If you choose to simply go with the flow, you often wind up going down the drain. On the other hand, if you plan the journey, and prepare your car for it and check it regularly, you will undoubtedly arrive. There are many dimensions to this journey, but the one I want to focus on here is, once again, your instrument. Your instrument on this journey is your automobile. The essential thing you do before any trip is your checkup. The checkup is the simple act of taking time out to put gas in your tank and see whether all the other systems are "go."

Why Bother Tuning Your Instrument?

In order for people to do anything, they need a compelling reason. Why do I think the first thing you should do every day is to tune your instrument? For the same reasons as a violinist tunes her instrument before a performance, and for the same reasons as you prepare your automobile for a journey.

You are a potential that needs to be actualized. How do you get to actualize your potential? By having the energy to do so, and by focusing your personal power. Both of these occur when you do the mental renewal exercise that you will learn in a minute. You will find that some incredible things will happen to you when you do this exercise regularly. First, your energy level will explode. Part of the reason is that your energy will not be siphoned off in bad feelings or worries, anxieties or stressful considerations. You will experience a sense of centeredness, an inner harmony, and you will discover what the words inner peace and serenity mean. Further, you will discover that your ability to focus, stay on task, and do the hard things that need to be done to get you where you want to go in life will be easier. Your creativity will unfold, and you will have a new openness to others and to the universe. You will have a calm and inner quietness that allows you to see life and its travails in better perspective. Your ability to handle the problems of living will grow daily, and you will never slip into a sense of powerlessness over the adversities that come your way. You will even discover that you look different, and others will come up to you and say, "I don't know what it is, but you have an inner glow and a sense of calm about you." This will occur because your face is the road map to your mind, your feelings, your beliefs.

When you do the mental exercise, you will see a number of interesting things happen to your body, all of which are measurable and have been validated scientifically. Your brain will start emitting alpha waves; these are the waves that have been associated with feelings of well-being, as well as with creativity. The lactic acid level in your blood will decline precipitously during a mental renewal exercise. Physicians have found that when a person is experiencing great stress, the lactic acid level in the blood goes up; conversely, when a person is experiencing a sense of quiet, the lactic acid level in the blood goes down. Further, when a person is upset, the heart beats faster. If that is chronic, the person may become a candidate for high blood pressure, and that can set him or her up for a heart attack, a stroke, or atherosclerosis, and even dispose him or her to cancer. During a mental renewal exercise, your heart slows down; you can measure this yourself by taking your pulse before and after doing the mental renewal exercise. Another interesting physiological change occurs, and that is to your skin. If a researcher put a galvanometer on your skin when you were experiencing stress, it would show that the surface of your skin becomes moist—that's how a lie detector works. During a mental renewal exercise, the surface of your skin dries up, and that is a sign that you are entering a stress-free state. One last way to prove that the mental renewal exercise is good for you is for you to do a mirror test. Simply look at yourself in a mirror before you do a mental renewal exercise; then, after you are done, look at yourself in the mirror again. What you see will be simply remarkable. The lines in your face will have softened; your complexion will appear more vivid; your eyes will shine like coals; a look of peacefulness will emanate from inside, and you will see it. That simple mirror test will give you prima facie evidence that something good has happened to you. Likewise, the other payoffs mentioned above, such as energy, focus, and drive, will all become self-evident in your experience.

How Do You Do It?

By now, you should be saying, "Teach me how to do it." It is really very simple. You sit in a chair, close your eyes, and for twenty minutes repeat to yourself, without using any vocal sounds, the word *yes*.

You're probably saying, "It's unbelievable; all the benefits recited above, and all you do is to say, yes, yes, yes, yes?'' Yes! It is unbelievable, but you don't have to believe anything; you can test it out. I think that if you do want to tune your instrument, actualize your potential, and not only be great in sales, but have a great life, then it is important to explore an area of your lived experience that can help catapult you there. Try it.

Let me explain the methodology and give you some reasoning behind the exercise. First of all, the ideal duration of an exercise is twenty minutes. Later I will show you know you can modify it. The exercise is really a profound time-out for your system—a rest. It is a quieting down process. Most of the time, in your active conscious awareness you are juggling about five balls at once, e.g., the client you're about to call on, the level of gas in your car, the problems you have with the factory, your spouse's present that you haven't bought yet, the monthly bills you haven't yet paid. This kind of ratiocination is going on all the time, and your mind is shifting from one topic to another, from your sense experiences, to memories, or to fragmented plans, to obligations—back and forth. You are bombarded with internal and external stimuli that compete to capture your attention; when you focus on one thing, other things intrude and break up your thought process. All this takes energy. On the other hand, during a mental renewal exercise, you are consciously focusing only on one thing, and that one thing is the word yes. The word yes is your focus vehicle. It gives your conscious mind a single focus of active attention. That single focus is perceived in your mind in a very quiet, soft, fluid, unemotional manner. It is pretty innocuous, pretty unstimulating, pretty bland. Yes, it is supposed to be. If I gave you as a focus vehicle, the words Marilyn Monroe or Robert Redford, you would have a focus vehicle that was lively, exciting, emotionally evocative, and visually stimulating. That might be fun, but it wouldn't renew you mentally. The word yes and the manner in which it is used in this exercise have a simple positive thrust. It was chosen because for most people it has a connotation that generates a benign but quiet forward momentum. Further, yes is abstract and not freighted with specific concrete memories, details, or emotions. What it does is give your conscious mind something to do while your body is winding down and your mind is getting refreshed and refocused. That something is supposed to be low key; in fact, it is more low key, i.e., less dynamic, than counting sheep. It provides a hook, or a focus, for your innate drive to attend to something. Another way to look at the yes is to think of it as a low-intensity anchor affirming all that is good. It does not have the emotional punch of yes! when you're using it as an anchor with the intent of putting yourself instantly into an achieving state.

So, the focus vehicle is yes. The word is repeated in your mind, slowly, over and over and over. The posture that you adopt as you are doing this is passive—simply let the recitation happen. The expression of the word is gentle, and the analogy to keep in mind is to let yourself *flow*. While you are moving through this repetitious process, other thoughts will come charging in. This is normal and expected. To handle this, when you become aware that you are thinking about your job, your kids, your time, your spouse, your finances, etc., *gently*, and I emphasize gently, go back to your focus vehicle, yes, and resume the repetitions.

As you are reciting your focus vehicle, do not make any audible sound; simply perceive it in your mind. See it either black on white or white on black; stick to one picture and one graphic image. Don't get creative by moving from black to red, from a Times Roman type to a sans serif or to longhand. Choose one visual image and stay with it. And if your visual imagination is not your strong suit, simply hear the yes or feel it. But keep the focus vehicle consistent. Be gentle and passive, don't force it, and don't get frustrated when other issues hop on your front burner of awareness. To repeat, *gently* go back to your focus vehicle. That's it; that's the method.

An Ideal Program

An ideal program would be to do this mental renewal exercise twice a day, once in the morning before breakfast and once in the late afternoon or early evening before dinner. Such a program would allow you to maximize the payoffs associated with mental renewal. However, I am a stark pragmatist, and I believe something is better than nothing. If you can't do it twice a day, do it once a day. If you can't do it for twenty minutes, do it for ten, or five, or even two. Something is better than nothing, and even a two-minute time-out can bring some refreshment.

Ideally, the mental renewal exercise would end with a *bridge*. When you finish a twenty-minute event, you will be in a state of deep relaxation, and it is a good idea to walk over a bridge to your active life, as opposed to going from a state of deep relaxation right into action. What is the bridge? You are still sitting in your chair and your eyes are still closed, but you stop your sound and start orienting yourself in your mind to what you are going to do next and for the rest of the day. Simply spend a minute or so reflecting on your plans. Then, at the end of this reflection, open your eyes and move into action.

Some Do's and Don'ts

Below is a list of do's and don'ts to keep in mind as you proceed with your mental renewal exercise. Most are self-explanatory, but afterwards I will comment on a number of them that may not be.

Do	*Don't*
Find regular times each day when you can do your MRE.	Don't do the MRE after eating—allow your food to be well digested; wait at least two hours after eating.
In the beginning, at least, find a quiet place to do your MRE.	Don't do your MRE lying down—you'll probably fall asleep.
Sit in a comfortable position with your head free.	Don't do your MRE with your head resting against a pillow or the back of a chair.
Loosen tight clothing, and, if you wish, take your shoes off.	Don't do your MRE next to a telephone or where sharp, loud, unexpected noises are likely to occur.

Close your eyes and simply listen to your breathing for a minute before you begin your MRE.

Consciously relax all your muscles.

Repeat, in your mind's eye, the focus vehicle you have chosen.

Expect thought and feeling intrusions, but when you become aware that you are not doing yes, *gently* go back to it.

Time your MRE with your watch. Open your eyes to check the time, to see if 15 to 20 minutes are up.

Have a two-minute bridge before moving into activity.

Look at yourself in a mirror before and after your MRE.

Do persevere because every MRE is a good MRE.

Don't time your MRE with an alarm clock.

Don't do your MRE immediately after exercise; allow your system to return to normal of its own accord.

Don't do your MRE late at night unless you want to stay up for a few hours.

Don't do your MRE while you are driving—it can be hazardous to your health!

Don't think that a good MRE means staying *rigidly* with your sound and excluding thoughts.

Don't abandon the practice of MRE because you omit it occasionally.

Don't feel that you are doing nothing during an MRE; just the reverse—you are doing the single best thing possible for yourself, your mind, your feelings, and your focus.

Why You Can't Do It and What to Do About It

A number of obstacles can arise that make it difficult for you to do your MRE regularly. The typical cry of frustration is, "I can't find the time." My reaction to this is that you can always find the time for the things that are truly important to you. You find time to eat every day; well, think of MRE as food for your mind, and just as you would not usually have a day without your proteins, carbohydrates, and vitamins, realize that MRE is the way to give your mind the nourishment it needs. I put this chapter early in the book for one reason, and that is because if I could teach you only one thing that could transform your life and your work, MRE is it. It is, in my judgment, the single most important ripple you can send through yourself. This ripple will touch every single area of your life in profound ways. It will help you feel great, put you into an achieving state, help you to accomplish all your goals in life, improve your health, make you a better salesman, improve your personal productivity. You will find that by investing the necessary time to do your MRE every day, you will accomplish vastly more in less time.

I do understand how busy you can be, but I also know that some parts of the day are more productive than other parts. MRE can keep you at a consistent high level of performance throughout the day.

Also, remember that there may be days when you have to omit it. Then do a modified version of it. It will keep you in practice, and you will still derive some benefit. Also, anytime you are waiting for someone—at an airport, at a doctor's office, outside a client's office—simply shut your eyes and do an MRE for as long or as brief a time as is available.

If you say, "I can't do it at home because I have little kids running around," all is not lost. When my two sons were tykes, my wife would watch them while I did my MRE, and then I would watch them while she did her MRE. A little cooperation can provide the time if you really want it.

Somebody else might say, "I couldn't possibly sit still for twenty minutes." Okay, if that is the case, start with only five minutes, then do seven, and progressively move up. Even if you are not comfortable going beyond eleven minutes, do eleven minutes. But do it regularly; do it consistently. Later, when I show you how to plan a day, I will offer a suggestion on how to keep MRE on your front burner.

Someone else might say, "When I try to sit quietly and do an MRE, it increases my anxiety." There is only a small minority of folks for whom this is true; for almost all others, MRE is a benign method to get calm and centered. If MRE does make you jumpy, you can do one of two things. You can work through it gently following the method, and see if by the end of twenty minutes you feel better—the odds are that you will detect a distinct improvement in your feeling state after you stop. On the other hand, I am a great believer in listening to the messages your body is sending. If you get an overwhelming headache, or break out in a sweat, or start hyperventilating, stop immediately. It may be that this method is not for you. I do, however, want to reiterate that this kind of experience is very rare. For most of you, stay with it and give it a fair trial.

There is one last question that is puzzling, and it is this: "Why do those folks who know how to do MRE and are convinced of its incredible value still find a way not to do it?" This is related to the business a person is in. Is it having a life that is filled with fun, laughter, service, enriching experiences, and love; or is it a life characterized by a lot of pain, guilt, anger, frustration, disappointment, and dreams that never materialized? The answer to that question is tested by a person's behavior. MRE is a behavior that can get you there. There are other ways, but this one is simple and a fast track to rippling waves that can be profound.

Summary and Bridge

Mental renewal exercise (MRE) is a simple and powerful way to give your mind and body a repair job. It can prepare a person to deal with the stresses of a day, restore depleted energy, create feelings of inner harmony, and unleash amazing creativity in the regular practitioner. A protocol spelling out the method is included, and a rationale for making this an integral part of your life is made.

The next chapter takes MRE and combines it with a deep motivation technique that can amplify a person's inner drive and allow mountains to be climbed with ease.

6

A Deep Motivation Technique: RAVE

	Yes	No
1. Is it important to you to follow through on your goals and plans?	☐	☐
2. It is important to you to overcome bad habits and replace them with life-enhancing ones?	☐	☐
3. Would you like to learn how to reprogram yourself so that you operate at a vastly more effective level?	☐	☐

In the previous chapter you learned how to do the mental renewal exercise (MRE). This was placed early in the book, and I remind you why again: because the place to start an improvement process is in your mind. What happens to most of us, as we are caught up in making a living and solving a myriad of other problems, is that almost on a daily basis we run out of time. For most busy people, their plate is not only full, it is overflowing. Hence, to find time to read a book like this, let alone do many of the exercises recommended, might appear to be unrealistic. But I want you to put a picture in your mind right now of a man cutting tree trunks into small logs that can fit into his stove. Winter is coming soon, but behind him is a mountain of tree trunks, and you hear him say, "I can't take time out to sharpen the saw." Most of us chuckle at the image, and smile at the shortsightedness of the man. We know that if he did take time out to sharpen his saw, he could go through the pile of tree trunks at a vastly swifter rate. We know, too, if he persists in trying to cut the tree trunks without sharpening his saw, it will get harder and harder, and he will get less productive because it will take longer and longer to do the job.

The solution to his problem is so self-evident that few of us need to think twice about it, but the fact of the matter is that many hard-driving folks out there in the marketplace do not take time out to sharpen their saw. As a consequence, many are operating on raw energy, get burnt out, his performance plateaus, rely on anesthesia breaks, and live lives of noisy desperation.

I have invited you to test out MRE; it is one of the most powerful methods of sharpening your saw on a daily basis that I know of. You can, however, using it as your jump-off point, tap into a number of other amazing powers that you have. I am referring to RAVE, a deep motivation technique. RAVE is a methodology that can truly transform your life, your beliefs, your feelings, and your habits and give you the impetus to accomplish goals that are important to you.

What Is RAVE?

RAVE is an acronym that means: Relaxation, Affirmation, Visualization, Emotionalization.

Relaxation

Relaxation is what occurs as a consequence of doing the MRE. The importance of putting yourself into a state of deep relaxation is that your mind goes into a state in which it is most amenable to accepting suggestions. It is a time when your mind can be effectively programmed or reprogrammed. It is a state in which you can plant in your mind directions, orders, wishes, dreams, goals, desires—anything you want. It is a state in which it is most likely that these directions will stick and, in fact, become a powerful driving force for making things happen. Why? Well, first of all, you are a goal-seeking, goal-achieving animal. You can do one of two things: You can let others tell you what your goals should be, accept them, and go after them; or you can decide that it is your life and you are going to do it your way. But what drives a person, what motivates a person, is having a clear, unambiguous picture of what it is that he or she wants. Goals that are vague, abstract, fuzzy, or generic do not, will not, and never have motivated anyone to do anything. When a person does not have crystal-clear goals, that person invariably becomes fixated on short-term, hedonistic, self-gratificatory, tension release preoccupations. Such a path does not typically lead to a life well lived.

Let's presume that you want to be great in sales and have a great life, for starters. How can you enhance your chances of doing this? Do RAVE on a regular basis. The relaxation step of the process is achieved by the same method used in doing the MRE. How long should you do it? Do it for ten minutes. For most people this is sufficient time to put them into a dive, quiet down, and allow the brain to start emitting alpha waves. For some it could take a little longer or a little less time; ten minutes is a ballpark figure suitable for most. After ten minutes you are in a position to do the A—affirmation.

Affirmation

An affirmation is a simple "I" statement that affirms that you are already in possession of that which you seek. The statement will be in the present tense or the present perfect tense. For example:

I have exceeded all my sales targets.
I can call on anybody fearlessly.
I can speak in public with poise and confidence.
I sharpen my saw every day.
I am in optimum good health.
I am an assertive person.
I weigh 159 pounds.
I am free from the need to smoke cigarettes.

I have a net worth in excess of $1 million.
I drive a Lexus SC 400.
I am a free spirit.
I have traveled around the entire globe.
I am in a terrific marriage.

It is a good idea to write down the affirmation you are going to use before you do RAVE. Keep it simple, and keep it short. Use the examples above as a model to imitate. As you can see, you can work on personality attributes that you want to have, material goals, bodily traits, or any goal of your choosing. Remember, this is your program, and you can sharpen the saw at any angle you wish.

How many times do you repeat this affirmation you have created? There is no fixed, magical number, but a guideline would be one affirmation every five seconds, or twelve in a minute, and twenty-four in two minutes. Let the affirmation step last approximately two minutes. It is not necessary to get compulsive about the precision. The guideline is ballpark, and if you do more or less, it is not a problem. Just make the process fluid, gentle, and hopeful.

Visualization

Here you tap your imagination. Here you become the director of the movie-making capability in your mind. Here you can give yourself permission to see vivid colors, hear loud sounds, feel textures, taste variations, and smell aromas—all in support of seeing and experiencing yourself in a possession of that which you want. If, for example, you want to be in optimum good health, in your mind's eye see yourself walking along a path in a park surrounded by the colors and odors of spring, and get a sense of how fit, alive, and energetic you feel as you move along. If you want a Lexus SC 400, see yourself behind the wheel driving swiftly down the highway, smelling the fresh leather smell of the upholstery, hearing the stereo play sweet music, and feeling just fine. If you want to speak in public with poise and confidence, see yourself standing in front of a group who are enraptured by what you are saying; see yourself explaining a position without any notes, using emphatic gestures and enjoying the experience. Try it with a goal of your own choosing.

How long do you do this? Approximately three minutes. Again, give yourself permission to get into it. Let the content of the picture flow out of the content of the affirmation, let the presentation be gentle and unforced, and go where it takes you.

Emotionalization

This is just a big word for making sure you inject *feeling* into the active part of your RAVE exercise, and that part is the AV part—the affirmation and visualization part. When you do your affirmation, invest it with positive, enthusiastic passion. Avoid affirming your goal in a bland, mental monotone, computer-like expression. That will not get in very deep at all. But freighting your affirmation with feeling, passion, enthusiasm, and optimism, conveyed with confidence and excitement, will mainline the affirmation into your mind and it will stick.

Likewise, during the visualization part of RAVE, invest it with passion and feel thrilled about being in possession of that which you want; now, as you are seeing the picture and feeling thrilled about it, make two fists, and say yes! You can make that iteration about five times also. What you are doing is stacking your anchors, really investing the dream with enthusiasm. The chances of making it happen are amazing.

Summary and Bridge

So, let's bring it together. Do RAVE at least once a day in a full-blown way, as an augmentation of one of your two MREs. Why only one of the MREs? Because it takes planning and more effort to do RAVE, and I do not want you to abandon MRE simply because you are not up to this. So one MRE a day is simply an MRE; then do one RAVE a day.

Also, just as with MRE, you can do RAVE in a modified version. If you collapse the time frames, but go through the four steps, the process will still have the power to get you moving—to keep the things that are truly important to you on the front burner.

You may wonder if you can do a different goal each day. Yes. You have a long life ahead, and it has many dimensions, so once you put a program in on a given day, you can move to another goal. Periodically you can go back and reinforce a particular goal in order to heighten the flame of passion and conviction.

The power of this process is that anything good or great first occurs in your mind. This process puts it there as an end result, and as with all goal achieving, the paradox is that you start at the end. With RAVE you get that dream in your mind vividly, with passion, feeling, enthusiasm, and conviction. This makes you a believer! Nothing good or great ever occurs if you don't believe it will.

So test it out. The results will become self-evident. You will be using a way to sharpen your saw that will, indeed, make your dreams come true.

The next chapter deals with your body and your health, and how to increase your aliveness, your energy, and even your longevity.

7

A Commitment to Optimum Good Health

	Yes	No
1. Do you want to live a long, healthful life?	☐	☐
2. Is having high energy and aliveness important to you?	☐	☐
3. Would you like to learn a simple regimen that would help profoundly to keep you in an achieving state?	☐	☐

As long as you are alive, your body is sending our ripples, and for most salespeople I know and have given seminars to, those ripples are not entirely positive. At the end of an all-day seminar for salespeople, for example, my clothes would be reeking with smoke, whereas other occupational groups would typically banish smokers to the outside. Salespeople must be aggressive, ambitious, and self-reliant, but all of these demands create great stress, which often gets combatted by the good life—filet mignons, martinis, and ulcers. Unfortunately, this short-term hedonism can lead to long-term health problems.

Your body is going to send out ripples one way or the other, so commit yourself to sending out positive ripples. It is something totally within your control. Why bother? Simply because when the ripples are positive, the payoffs in every other area of your life are colossal. In order to have compelling reasons to do the right things to achieve optimum good health, the rationale needs to be spelled out. But you need to consider the pain first, the pain that comes when you choose to live a life in which taking care of your body is *not* a high priority.

The Pain to Be Experienced

To motivate you to optimum good health, I want you to focus on the pain you will experience if you choose to ignore and abuse your health. Why? Because pain is the great motivator. People will do more to avoid pain, discomfort, or inconvenience than they will do to reap the positive, life-giving benefits of doing the right things. This is true with respect not only to health, but to everything. If you're serious about having a great life, then really get into the pain you will experience if you let your body go. It helps to create what I call good guilt.

Review the statistics on the killing diseases: heart attack, stroke, athlerosclerosis—salespeople are familiar with them. As awesome as the statistics are, something is lost in them; they are impersonal, unemotional, only numbers. To get motivated, it's necessary for you to personalize them. How? Reflect on your past experience and answer these questions: Have you ever been sick in your life? Have you ever been incapacitated as a result of injury? A yes means that you have some understanding of what it's like to be out of action. Let me give you a few other prompters to think about:

- How did the sickness or injury affect your appearance?
- How did it affect your self-image?
- How did you feel about your sickness or injury?
- Reflect on the physical pain.

- How did it affect your will to live?
- How did it affect your relationships with the people you care for?
- How did it affect your ability to sell?
- How did it affect your energy level?
- How did it affect your ability to focus?
- How did it affect your attitudes?
- What things did you want to do that you were not able to?
- What places did you want to go to, but couldn't?
- How did it affect your pocketbook?
- What opportunities did you lose?
- How much of your most precious irreversible resource, time, did you lose?
- How did it affect your sex life?

Respond to each one of these questions because they can help you get in touch with your pain. While you do it, step back and turn on your creative imagination, and bring back the memory as vividly as you can. See yourself in pain; feel the pain once again; hear the sounds that were circulating about you at the time; smell the smells that permeated the environment; feel the feelings. Remember the scenes. Get into it.

Those scenes are only a prelude of what is to come if you do not commit yourself to optimum good health. Except, in all likelihood, it will be worse and eventually become chronic, which could lead ultimately to an early demise.

While you are at it, let's consider what a too early demise means. Reflect on what would not happen if you died ten, twenty, or thirty years before your genetic number was up.

- Where are the places you never would travel to?
- Who are the little children you would never dandle on your knee?
- What are the experiences you never would have?
- What are the stories you would never tell?
- Who are the precious ones you would never see again?
- Whose hands would you never hold again?
- With whom would you never go for a walk again?
- Who would you never make love to again?

Prescinding from sickness for a minute, reflect on your body when it is totally out of shape. What is your stamina level? How do you look? What is your muscle tone like? How strong are you? What is your waist size? Look at your belly. Look at your behind. What do others think of your appearance? How do you feel knowing others are able to jog for more than a mile?

Have You Had Enough?

OK. This chapter is not meant to depress you. It is meant to give you absolutely compelling reasons to get it together. If you answered the questions above, you're partially there. Why only partially? Because now you need to get in touch with the positive ripple effects that optimum good health would have, if you did have it. So, answer these questions:

- How would you look if you were in optimum good health? Focus on different parts of your body, slowly. Make the picture vivid, and get in touch with your feelings as you move from one focus to the next: Your stomach? Your arm muscles? Your thigh and calf muscles? Your waist size? Your weight? Your behind? Your dress/suit size?
- How would others think you looked?
- How would your endurance be?
- How would your blood pressure be?
- How would your skin tone be?
- How would you feel?
- How often would you get sick?
- What would your energy level be like?

Elaborate on these payoffs. Project yourself into the future, relating to the people who are special to you. See yourself productive, learning, growing, traveling, laughing, and enjoying a long, full life.

Now put the whole picture together, and get a real sense of how positively thrilled you are about your new body. Again, see it vividly; feel it; hear yourself and others commenting on it. Breathe deeply while you're holding this picture in your mind, smile, and as you hold this sweet picture in your mind, say loudly, while squeezing your fists, yes! And say it again. And again. And again. And again.

What Have You Done?

If you have followed to this point, you have now gotten in touch with compelling reasons to commit yourself to optimum good health. You've experienced the pains you will undergo if you do not change, and you have experienced the positive pleasures and rewards you will reap when you do achieve optimum good health. Further, with the last exercise above, you have anchored yourself into a positive commitment to do so. All you will have to do in the future to reignite your motivation is to simply say yes! while squeezing your fists, and the desire to achieve it will return. Motivation is the hard part, and, as you know, it is *not* something that you get once and then have for ever. Periodically reflect on the pains associated with couch potatoism, regularly see yourself in your mind's eye being the ideal you want to be, and use your anchor, yes!, every day.

What Next?

Once you're motivated, it is necessary to have a program that is doable. The program below is just that. It is designed for busy salespeople, who are constantly on the move, work long hours, and never have enough time. It has five parts:

1. Take an antioxidant pill.
2. Breathe diaphragmatically.
3. Eat properly.
4. Exercise aerobically.
5. Strengthen muscles.

Number one is a no-brainer. It takes exactly thirteen and one-half seconds to twist open a bottle, fetch a glass of water, and pop a pill (I timed it!). Numbers two and three you already do—so just learn to do them right. Number 4 is not awesome at all. Once you get out of bed, you already are putting your body in motion, and that is a plus. All you need to do is find a minimum of fifteen minutes to walk every day and you've got it. Number five you will discover you can do anywhere. All you need to do is take advantage of the opportunity, and recognize that anything is better than nothing.

Take an Antioxidant

The latest research shows that a major contributing cause of heart attack, stroke, atherosclerosis, cancer, and other diseases is free radicals. Free radicals are molecules in the blood that are starved for oxygen. They get their oxygen by attacking healthy cells that have it, and in that act they destroy the cell. As the number of free radicals in a person's blood goes up, the probability of acquiring one of these killing diseases increases. The free radicals come from the fatty foods we eat, inhaled smoke, a sedentary lifestyle, and a shallow breathing style that underoxygenates the blood. When this lifestyle occurs, free radicals proliferate in the blood, and the cells do not have enough resistance to ward off their attacks.

What is part of the solution? Each day take antioxidant vitamins. Antioxidants throw up a protective shield around cells and prevent the free radicals from stealing the oxygen they need to survive. When the free radicals don't get the oxygen they need to survive, they die. The healthy cells are left alone and function in the manner they are supposed to. There are many antioxidants on the market, but the most powerful ones are vitamin E, vitamin C, and vitamin A (beta-carotene). In the dosage the experts recommend, they are harmless. A generally agreed-upon quantity is the following:

Vitamin E 400 I.U.
Vitamin C 500 mg
Beta-carotene 25,000 I.U.

To simplify taking these, vitamin companies have combined them into an antioxidant formula pressed into one tablet. Ask for an ACE tablet. The person at your health food store will know exactly what you want and probably will show you a number of different ones to choose from.

Some physicians believe that the discovery of the role antioxidants play in neutralizing the destructiveness of free radicals is the single most important medical and nutritional discovery in the last fifty years. The research is building every day, and articles supporting antioxidants' use and efficacy across a broad range of diseases are appearing in the accepted medical journals. It may take five more years before orthodox medicine gives its unqualified endorsement, but there is no good reason to wait. The research that has been done so far on animals and on humans is overwhelming in demonstrating positive outcomes. In the dosages mentioned above, these vitamins are harmless. If you have any reservation, clear it with a knowledgeable physician.

In *Prevention*, February 1994, a number of giants in the field of nutrition were asked what daily supplements they took themselves. This is what a number of them responded:

- William Castelli, M.D., Director of Framingham Heart Study—500 mg vitamin C, 400 I.U. vitamin E, 1 mg folate, 1 multivitamin.
- Walter Willett, M.D., Dr. P.H., Professor of Epidemiology and Nutrition, Harvard University School of Public Health—400 I.U. vitamin E, 1 multivitamin.
- James W. Anderson, M.D., Chief, Metabolic-Endocrine Section, Veterans Administration, and Professor of Medicine and Clinical Nutrition, University of Kentucky—15 mg beta-carotene, 1000 mg vitamin C, 400 mg vitamin E.
- Dean Ornish, M.D., Director, Preventive Medicine Research Institute, Sausalito—3000 mg vitamin C, 1 multivitamin (includes 3 mg beta-carotene and 100 I.U. vitamin E).
- Kenneth Cooper, M.D., President and Founder, Cooper Clinic, Dallas—1000 mg vitamin C, 400 I.U. vitamin E, 15 mg beta-carotene.

Although most doctors will tell you to forget supplements and eat a balanced diet, increasing numbers of experts on nutrition, the heart, oncology, and endocrinology are taking supplements themselves because they realize that it is very difficult to get the levels you need just from diet. Take a look at these giants in the field, and think about what they do themselves. That can help you make a decision.

So step one in the five-part program to achieve optimum good health is: Take an ACE antioxidant tablet every day from now on.

Breathe Diaphragmatically

Most folks starve themselves of the one thing that can lead to vibrant health, explosive energy, and cells functioning properly, and that is oxygen. Oxygen is necessary for two reasons: It stimulates the cells in your body to produce ATP (adenosine triphosphate), and it stimulates the lymphatic system. ATP is the fuel that powers all your cells and organs. If oxygen intake is low, ATP production will be low, and the body will become a candidate for disease. If breathing is impaired, if the environment is polluted, or even if breathing is habitually shallow, the person takes in less oxygen on an inhalation, and the result is less ATP, which lowers levels of energy and leads to a higher incidence of disease.

We have a system in our bodies that is called the lymphatic system. The lymphatic system is sometimes referred to as the body's waste disposal system. Lymph is the fluidic substance that surrounds every cell in the body. It carries off the waste that the cells generate in the process of producing ATP. Oxygen is what stimulates the lymph to do what it is supposed to do. When oxygen intake levels are low, impaired functioning of the lymphatic system occurs, and this can predispose a person to all kinds of diseases.

How can you address this problem and maximize your oxygen? The answer is deep breathing, or, more technically, diaphragmatic breathing. How can you know if you are doing diaphragmatic breathing? Do this exercise. Put your right hand on your chest, and your left hand on your abdomen, just above your navel. Now, as you take a deep breath in through your nose, drive the air low into your abdomen so that your left hand rises as your belly expands. If you're doing it right, your right hand has not moved. The classic Marine Corps way of breathing, with stomach in chest out, is not diaphragmatic breathing. In fact, that kind of breathing is shallow breathing and is not designed to get you the kind of oxygen you really need.

Now, while you're at it, let's do a few more iterations of deep breathing with your right hand on your chest and your left hand on your abdomen. Sometimes it is called belly breathing. Don't worry, your belly will not become permanently distended—just the opposite; you are actually exercising and strengthening your stomach muscles by diaphragmatic breathing.

Now let's do it a little more systematically, and inhale, hold, then exhale in the following ratio: 1:4:2. For example, if you inhale through your nose for a five count, you will hold the breath for a count of twenty, and exhale through the mouth for a count of ten, totally deflating your lungs. Try it out. If a five-count inhalation is too much for you, try a four-count inhalation, sixteen hold, and eight exhale. Or if you're a smoker and haven't had a good breath in a long while, try a three-, twelve-, and six-count routine. If, on the other hand, you can take a deeper and longer inhalation without experiencing discomfort, try a 6:24:12.

While you do deep breathing, listen to the messages your body is sending. If you get dizzy or nauseous or develop a headache, back off immediately and breathe the way you normally breathe. Just inhale for the count of one and exhale without trying to hold your breath at all. When your distress signals pass, you can still breathe deeply and diaphragmatically. Just don't hold your breath, and slowly improve the duration of your inhalation at another time. Eventually, with practice and close monitoring, you will be able to move back to the 1:4:2 ratio of inhale, hold, and exhale.

What's So Important About the Routine

First of all, inhaling through your nose allows you to take in more air from the atmosphere than inhaling through your mouth. Second, if you repeatedly inhale through your mouth, your mouth cavity dries up rapidly, and in no time your throat gets irritated. Third, it is easier to drive the air into the lower reaches of your abdomen when the breath is taken in through the nose. And last, breathing diaphragmatically through the nose is more comfortable than deep breathing through the mouth.

Why then hold the breath? The reason is that it allows more of the oxygen that is taken in to get into the blood system. If we breathed in a very shallow fashion, some of the oxygen that we breathed in would go right out on the exhalation, and thus the body would benefit from only a small part of that oxygen intake. We hold the breath for four times the inhalation in order to let the oxygen permeate the cells more fully.

What is the purpose of the exhalation? The exhalation is your body's prime disposer of waste. If an exhaled breath were captured in a test tube and examined microscopically, you would probably faint to see what is coming out of your mouth all day. What you would see are toxins, waste, refuse your body is throwing off from the transactions that occur between blood, cells, and lymph. If you could not exhale, you would die in short order. The reason for exhaling for twice as long as the deep inhalation is that it allows more waste to be expelled from your body.

To summarize: the more oxygen you take in each day, the more ATP your body produces, and the higher will be your energy level and level of health. The longer you can comfortably hold your breath after an inhalation, the more fully oxygenated your cells will get. The longer your exhalation after a deep diaphragmatic breath, the more toxins will get expelled from your body. Now, in order to put some reasonable boundaries around these generalizations, what regimen might I suggest? Each day take ten deep diaphragmatic breaths at three different times of the day. To remember the protocol, simply keep in mind "10X-3X."

What will be the payoff? Your energy will explode. This will become so self-evident that you won't need a dozen scientific studies to reinforce it. In fact, you will wonder why you never did it before. Where can you do it? You can do it driving to and from work, or on the train or bus; at your desk; while walking, standing, sitting; while you're listening on the telephone, attending a meeting, waiting, resting; or at break time, lunch time, dinner time; or while watching TV or listening to music—wherever! You have to breathe anyway, so at least three times a day attend to it, and breathe deeply.

Once you have started the routine above, do not limit yourself to thirty deep breaths a day. In fact, if you routinely got into the habit of diaphragmatic breathing and breathed that way most of the time, your energy would hardly ever flag. Test it out, and see what you discover.

Eat Properly

My goal is not to make you an expert on nutrition, but to suggest a set of guidelines that are doable, with payoffs for following them that will be so manifest that they will become the source of motivation to continue. First of all, there is a proven correlation between what people eat, what diseases they get, and how long they live. The body of scientific opinion is clearly on the side of fruits and vegetables, low fat, and meals with complex carbohydrates. What regimen can you follow without counting calories, milligrams of fat, or developing a long list of acceptable/unacceptable foods? From now on, let your rule of thumb be 70–30. As an ideal to aspire to, make 70 percent of what you consume each day be fruits and vegetables. Why does this make sense? Because your body is 65 percent water, and your cells need the fluidity that water gives it to function at an optimum level. Fruits and vegetables are water-content foods, and they are loaded with all the vitamins, minerals, and proteins that your body needs. A diet that is lopsided with non-water-content foods, like that of most people in the West, can cause plaque buildup in the arteries, lower energy levels, heart attack, stroke, and certain kinds of cancer. So test out 70–30. It's important not to be anal-compulsive about the guideline, because that orientation can boomerang. See the 70–30 as a guideline to aspire to whenever possible. If you do 50–50, 60–40, 40–60, or even 20–80 on a given day, don't abandon the idea. Just keep it there, and let it serve the purpose of being a source of good guilt. Approach the whole matter of eating flexibly with an eye to the long-term payoff.

What might be a few tips to support the goal? Every lunch or dinner you have, see if you can have a salad. Periodically order or cook an all-vegetable meal, and start falling in love with the diversity of tastes among the vegetables. For snacks, eat fruit, not chips, peanuts, ice cream, or candies. While you are eating the fruit, eat it slowly, savor the taste, roll it around your mouth, get in touch with its healthful goodness, and let the pleasure last. Last, remember what an old sage once said: "What you don't buy, you can't eat." And, of course, what you don't have in the house, you can't eat; so when you shop, buy a diversity of fruits and vegetables to have available at home.

You will soon discover that you are eating a lot, gaining less weight, and feeling more energetic. Once again, test it out.

Exercise Aerobically

There are three good reason to exercise aerobically every day. First, your heart is a muscle, and like all the muscles in your body, if you don't use it, you lose it, which is to say that when muscles are not exercised, they weaken and atrophy. In order to handle the physical and psychological emergencies that occur every day of your life, you need to have a heart that can respond to the demands. How can you strengthen your heart? Exercise. Second, in the course of exercising aerobically, you are forced to breathe deeply and take in more oxygen than normal. You know the importance of nourishing your cells with oxygen, and exercise is a great way to do just that. Third, you have a system in the body, mentioned earlier, called the lymphatic system; it is the body's waste disposal system. Lymph fluid surrounds every cell in the body and enables the body to take in nutrients and dispose of wastes that are created as the cells break down oxygen and create ATP. Since the lymphatic system does not have a pump like the circulatory system has, it gets activated by two things, oxygen and movement. Exercise thus provides the vehicle for helping it do what it is supposed to do. Also, as a further payoff on top of increased energy, deep breathing helps the lymphatic system to function more effectively.

Okay, what is a reasonable *minimalist* exercise regimen? Every day do fifteen minutes of continuous aerobic exercise. For how long? For the rest of your life. You choose the kind of aerobic exercise, and make it something you enjoy. In this instance pain is not the great motivator—just the opposite. Walk, swim, stroll, jog, trampoline, cut your grass with a lawn mower, etc. And vary it periodically in order to avoid boredom.

Strengthen Your Muscles

If you do aerobic exercise every day, you have a great start and will certainly strengthen your heart muscle and your leg muscles. To augment that—and, again, this is a minimalist program—get yourself two five-pound dumbbells. Each day exercise a few minutes, curling, lifting, and tensing your arm, shoulder, and chest muscles. To this regimen add this stomach- and back-strengthening exercise: Lie flat on your back, place your arms across your chest, raise your knees so that your legs are in a vee with respect to the ground, and lift your head off the floor as if to touch your chin to your upper chest. You will immediately feel the tension in your stomach and, in a little while, in your back. Do your age in repetitions every day. You may have to start out with five or ten—that's okay. Of course, if you are up to it, exceed your age in repetitions.

You can go to whatever heights you want with muscle-strengthening exercises. If you go beyond this minimalist program, get the advice of a professional trainer.

The end result of this effort will be stronger muscles, a flat stomach, fewer injuries, and more stamina—to say nothing of improved appearance.

Caveats: The Be-Carefuls

Before you embark on any of the protocols above, it would be prudent to have a physical checkup done by your physician. This will give you the green light to begin a lifestyle change. As you adopt a regimen that makes sense for you, it is important that you listen to the messages your body is sending you. Any pain, dizziness, nausea, or unsettled feeling is a message to stop what you are doing. Attempting to work through the pain is imprudent—stop, slow down, reassess. What we have here is only one path to fitness, and although most folks will flourish with it, you may not. In that case, try something else. Within the boundaries of deep breathing, right eating, effective exercise, vitamin supplementation, and muscle strengthening, there are many other possibilities. But, get on with it, and, to quote myself, "Do it now; do it when you don't feel like it; do it especially when you don't feel like it."

Summary and Bridge

A simple protocol for better health is spelled out. It deals with proper eating, exercise, breathing, antioxidants, and muscle strengthening. Everyone knows what happens to the quality of one's life when sickness strikes. Following this protocol, the chances of achieving optimum good health are the payoff.

The next chapter deals with the unique human power—choice. It is the power that, when exercised properly, leads to self-evident rewards and emboldens a person to continue to make more right choices.

8

Choice and Focus

	Yes	No
1. Is it important to you to know how to exercise your most unique human power?	☐	☐
2. Would you be interested in knowing why people go down one path rather than another?	☐	☐
3. Would you like to learn how to motivate yourself to do the right things in your life, your career, and your relationships?	☐	☐

Free choice is the unique human power. It is the decision to do this or that. Choice implies options and the ability to select the path you want. Most people have this ability most of the time, and it is the basis for our criminal justice system. The choices you make in life lead to action, and action leads to certain consequences. The law says that each person is responsible for the consequences of his or her behavior. This is true for you and for me. In fact, I would go so far as to say that you are where you are today as a consequence of all the choices you have made in your life. Right now, you are reaping the consequences of those choices: your social class, your education level, your occupation, your marital status, etc. Although most folks would agree with the previous statement, there are significant numbers of people who believe that we are prede-termined to certain kinds of lives, that we do not have the freedom to choose what we want to do with our lives. I would agree that in some parts of the world and under some profound situations of abuse, the kinds of choices one can make are extremely limited, but I believe that even then, human beings can always choose the meaning they are going to attach to a situation and their reaction to it.

So, I am asserting that basically you do have the power to choose. But the interesting question, in my judgment, is less whether you do or do not have the power than *why* we choose to go down one path as opposed to another.

I believe that there is an innate drive on the part of each person to seek satisfaction or happiness. But each person is confronted with a variety of possibilities that he or she can take advantage of to achieve that end. Why then, to repeat, does a person choose one path as opposed to another? I think that when a choice is about to be made, there is a lightning-fast calculation that goes on that assays the amount of pleasure to be gained as compared to the amount of pain that will be experienced from doing something or not.

Each option you have will lead to painful or rewarding pay-offs. If the choice is between pleasure and pain, pleasure will win out. If the choice is between a certain pain and a greater pain, the lesser pain will win out. However, the intriguing things about human nature is that pain is the great motivator, or, to be more precise, avoiding pain is the great motivator. I alluded to this ear-lier when discussing compelling reasons to commit to the goal of optimum good health.

Pain Is the Great Motivator

I have just spent seven chapters showing you how to celebrate yourself, feel good all the time, get enthusiasm, wind down, and, as a result, get yourself into an achieving state. In my judgment, all these ideas are true and incredibly valuable. It is important, however, to understand how humans behave and why they typically don't do one-tenth of what they could do. Further, it is important to understand why salespeople don't do one-tenth of what they already know how to. It is important to know why salespeople develop call reluctance, procrastinate, plateau out, accept third-rate performance from themselves, and don't make half the appointments they could. It's important to have a clear understanding of why there is so much smoking, drinking, golf in the afternoons, movie matinees, promiscuity, and fixation with toys—cars, labels, real estate, baubles, etc. When you don't know why, their lure is like a siren or a Circe beckoning you to her arms.

The reason is very simple: People don't like pain, don't enjoy pain, and will do more to avoid pain than anything else. What is pain? Pain is a subjective judgment a person makes about something. Pain is not out there. It's between the ears. Pain is a belief, an interpretation of an experience or potential experience. Pain is a conclusion that a person makes about something. It is something with a heavy negative valence. It is a meaning that a person has attached to a course of action. Our experiences as human beings just *are*, until we attach a valence to them—positive or negative, good or bad. Although the words may not be articulated overtly, or be on the front burner of active consciousness, the judgment sounds like this: "It's bad; it's awful; it's painful; it hurts; it's uncomfortable; it's unsettling; it's inconvenient; it's irritating; it's an imposition; it's tough; it's embarrassing; it's too time-consuming; it's no fun; it's too demanding, etc." When a person *defines* something as bad, negative, or hurtful, this becomes the motivation to avoid it.

So, if I am a salesperson and I define cold calling as a pain, for me it will be. If I find prospecting an irritation, I won't do it. If I define accurate paperwork as an imposition, I won't do it. If I find that planning my day carefully is not my thing, I won't do it. If I say that cold calling is an enormous headache, I will avoid doing it. If I find that calling on new prospects is no fun, I'll spend my time calling on old friends. If I believe that cross-selling is more trouble than it's worth, I won't bother. And if I believe that any or all of the above are true, and I do them anyway and experience the pain attached to the behavior, I will be one depressed, miserable wretch. Unless I have some constructive way to deal with this self-imposed stress, I will start thrashing about for ways to kill the pain, and find anesthetics that will help.

Anesthetics

You know some of the anesthetics, but let's think about them for a minute. Smoking is a neat anesthetic, except it kills, shortens lives, and disposes a smoker to higher probabilities of chronic disease. Drinking is a predictable way to numb oneself, and what does drinking do? It clearly puts one into a nonachieving state and lowers one's productivity, and, like smoking, alcoholism is a disease and disposes a person to higher rates of every other kind of disease. Food and indiscriminate eating, like rare steaks, sugars, desserts, candy bars, junk foods, and other high-fat addictions, lead to obesity, lower energy levels, and higher rates of chronic disease. Drugs like Valium, cocaine, crack, heroin, or even Prozac do indeed kill the pain, but as with all the other anesthetics, the probability of addiction is high. Apart from the hurtful side effects of all of these anesthetics, they put a person into a nonachieving state, smother creativity, maim a person's problem-solving ability, mask the real problem, and provide at best only temporary relief, a temporary respite, an interlude, a high, a buzz, a euphoria, a solace that doesn't last. What happens after the effects of the anesthetic wear off? The pain again rears its ugly head, and again, the longing for relief through anesthesia becomes the path of choice, the path of least resistance, the path to which a person has attached less pain.

Part of the reason people go down these paths is because they have the ability to choose. Having this ability enables people to avoid pain at all costs or, if they are confronted with two painful courses of action, to choose the less painful one. So, what do you know? You know that people's great motivation is to avoid pain, and you know that they have the power to choose which path they will go down.

The big question is, how can you get yourself motivated to do the right things in your life, in your job, in your career? The way I would do it is to examine the pain that you have attached to certain goals and appropriate courses of action. I would then change the the meanings of those actions so that they are no longer painful but positively rewarding, realize that by *not* doing them you will experience a greater pain, and burn that greater pain into your brain. Thus, since you are fundamentally not into pain, and will do more to avoid pain than anything else, you will be motivated to do the right things, and get into and stay in an achieving state.

You may think that this fixation on pain is negative thinking, but I can assure you that positive thinking, or a fixation on the payoffs of a behavior, is not enough. It's necessary, but it is not sufficient. By having your rewards and your pains in your active awareness when contemplating a course of action, you have a necessary and sufficient rationale for doing something. The pluses and the minuses give you a compelling "why." The reason why avoiding pain is the great motivator is that the act of avoiding and not experiencing something defined as pain is a reward. So we could, indeed, say that people are fundamentally into pleasure. But the way most get there is *more* by avoiding pain than by going after things that are positively rewarding. Thus, folks are basically motivated by rewards, and, therefore, we are not into negative thinking at all, but just the reverse.

We need not get tied up in this mental jujitsu. Let's apply the analysis to selling. Let's take cold calling. There are two kinds, by telephone and in person. Suppose you are cold calling a prospect for an appointment by telephone. Suppose you know that picking up the telephone and getting an appointment is the start of your sell cycle. If you want to demotivate yourself with respect to the calling, all you have to do is keep reminding yourself how much you hate doing it. Continue running the tape: "I hate it; I hate it; I hate it." Guaranteed, after a while either you won't do it or, if you do it, it will be half-hearted; you'll be calling the weather or your local sex line, or spending a lot of time with 800 or 900 numbers, to provide some relief, and you'll play games with yourself about the number of actual calls you made or, if you have to report your cold calling to a boss, lie about the process.

Okay, how can you redefine this experience so it is not painful? Think about the pain you will experience if you do not make the phone calls. Face up to it. If you don't do it, you don't get any appointments. No appointments, no interviews; no interviews, no identification of a real prospect; no prospects, no sales; no sales, no commissions, and pretty soon no job; no job, no money to pay your bills, such as your rent or mortgage, and pretty soon you have to move and get a tent. You're embarrassed; you feel guilty; you're angry at yourself; you see that you are yellow, that you have no courage, that you are a loser, and that other people think you are a loser too. Folks don't like to be around losers, and they start avoiding you. Your misery gets to your body; you have pains, you're fatigued, you have pains across your shoulders, you have migraines, and inside you hurt. After a while you become so strapped with your self-hatred that you just want to scream. Your spouse begins to hate you, and defines you as a lily-livered, spineless, useless wimp. Your children are embarrassed to let anyone know you are their parent.

Get into that pain you will be experiencing if you do not make your cold calls. Make it vivid; follow the logical chain of causality to more and greater pain. Feel it, see it, sense it, picture it, and realize it is yours—all you need to do is to avoid your cold calls. Once you have spent a little time reflecting on the pain you would experience if you don't make your cold calls, spend an equal amount on time on the positive payoffs you will accrue when you do, indeed, make the cold calls—e.g., cold calls, appointments, qualified prospects, presentations, sales closed, quota hit, increased commissions, money, the respect and admiration of your boss, your spouse, your children, the internal satisfaction that you are making it happen, the positive feelings of enthusiasm you get flooded with, the acute sense that you are making progress towards your other goals in life (the opportunities for growth, the toys, your travels, and enriching experiences). All of these are advanced by picking up that phone and making the calls.

What the exercise above gives you, and your mind, is a compelling answer to the question, why should I make these calls? When you get the answer to that "why" for anything you want or have to do, you will do it. It is worth the time to go through such a little reflection to motivate yourself to do anything—a vivid recitation of the pains and pleasures will provide you with the motivation.

Pleasure/Pain Attached to Your Self-Worth

Go back to the invitation to be a 10. Reflect on the pain you would avoid if you saw yourself as a 10, or the pain you will undoubtedly experience if you persist in seeing yourself as anything less than a 10. What would the pain look like? Reflect slowly and vividly on what is coming, and let your senses picture these images starkly.

You will be sad a lot, angry a lot, unfocused a lot, and dissipated frequently. You will discover that you often waste time, that you spend a lot of time being a spectator in life, watching TV and movies with actors getting high on their profession. You will be a procrastinator; you will accept the middle-class style of life dealt to you. You will spend your money on the lottery and your time waiting—waiting for your ship to come in. You'll put on weight, become old before your time, have a low propensity to take any risks; you won't have much adventure, fun, or peaks of experience in your life; you will do a lot of muddling through. "How are you?" people will ask. "I'm getting by," will be your response. Nobody will be close to you, and you will feel alone a lot; you will find you're jealous of those that have made it; and to top it off, you will get sick frequently, probably smoke, drink too much, and rarely smile. Inside you will know that you are afraid that someone is going to find out what a lowlife scum you really are, and your feelings of guilt and self-hatred will be reflected on your face. In no time you will be old and crusty and drool at the mouth, and when you die no one will miss you. About the only thing that you will be known for is your potential, potential that never became actual—a waste of all that oxygen you consumed, and now a pitiful excuse for fertilizer.

I hope you have had enough! Now, reflect again on all those experiences that are yours when you do live life from the vantage point of a 10. Think about your lightness of spirit, your positive feelings of joy, enthusiasm, serenity, control. Think of yourself making goals, executing plans, and creating your special destiny. Think of the adventure, the laughter, the good times, the friends, the travels, the service, the contributions you make. Think of how you look—your body, your face, your waistline—your energy level, your good health. Think about the ease with which you do the hard things, which are no longer hard, like cold calling. See yourself as fearless, full of courage, and absolutely unable to be intimidated. See yourself operating with the stark conviction that you don't have to prove anything, that you already are somebody. Feel the feelings, and feel thrilled about your 10ness.

When you spend time on both sides of the ledger, pain and pleasure, you will have compelling reasons to do whatever it is you want to do in life. And what is mind blowing is that when you do them, the ease and aplomb you exhibit will become your trademark, and embolden you to do even more.

Short Term, Long Term, and Focus

Okay, so now you know why people do what they do. They are into pleasure, ease, comfort, and happiness, and for most people the first order of business is to avoid pain, inconvenience, awkwardness, and hard work. One ineluctable consequence of this orientation is that folks get fixated on the near term and abandon the long term. Now is the time for pleasure, for fun, for comfort, for convenience, for satisfying the demands of the body and the senses. Tension release is the order of the day, anesthetic the prescription, and the result is observable everywhere—poverty and mediocrity where hedonistic self-gratification rules. What happens to an individual caught up in this? Opportunity is lost, ignored, denied, and, in fact, in many cases not even seen. Personal growth does not occur, potential is never actualized, goals are never set, and nothing significant happens in the life of a person preoccupied with tension release. Just the opposite: irresponsibility, fraud, criminality, self-abuse, and chaotic interpersonal relations occur. Families in which it is the dominant role of adapting to life disintegrate, become dysfunctional, and become breeding grounds for sociopaths, who repeat the same cycle in the next generation.

Salespeople don't tend to go to these extremes, but if you ever really investigate why a salesperson who does have opportunity does not perform up to expectations, you will find that he or she spends a disproportionate amount of time on self-gratification and tension release, as opposed to the steady execution of a sales plan.

Please don't get me wrong—I'm all for pleasure, self-gratification, fun, and comfort, but there needs to be a proper balance if one is to grow and maximize one's chances to be happy throughout one's lifetime. The quality of tomorrow's existence is a consequence of the choices we make today. What happens when one has no goals, dreams, or visions of a better future? The short-term, hedonistic, self-gratification life is all that is left. A person caught up in this literally never gets off the launching pad, or the couch. What do people need? Long-term goals about which they have a passion. If you have no goals nothing good or great will occur. The short term is the fixation. What is necessary? A balance between the short term and the development of long-term goals. In Chapter 21 I will present a format for crystallizing them. But let's consider the process that can make it possible.

The Key to Maintaining the Balance

The key to maintaining the balance between the short and long term, between here-and-now pleasure and long-term pleasure, between a life characterized by hedonistic tension release and the step-by-step progress toward personal growth and a life of superior service and achievement, is *focus.*

Once you acknowledge that you have the power to choose, to choose what you want to be, what you want to have, and what you want to experience; once you understand and embrace the idea that choice is the key to your self-empowerment, then you need to look into one critical step in the process that will dictate whether anything good or great will happen in your life, and if so, what. What you choose is among the alternatives presented to your mind. Your mind can choose only from the things you are paying attention to. What you are paying attention to, holding in your conscious awareness, is a choice. However, what you choose to focus on is the first step in having momentum work for you or against you. Your ultimate personal power flows out of the realization that you can choose what you want to focus on. What you do focus on fills up your mind and generates supporting actions. For example, suppose I have discovered in the past that chocolates taste great. If I hold chocolates in my mind, pretty soon the pleasures of chocolates will become apparent; focusing on the pleasures, then, leads to behavior that allows me to acquire chocolates.

This is true for anything moralists describe as a temptation—if you hold it in your mind, the pleasures capture the mind, and behaviors are set in motion that lead to the experience fantasized.

So the key to controlling your life, your feelings, your behavior is to control what you focus on. What you focus on starts the momentum, which, as you know, can become imperious once it starts. This is fine if it is something you really want to do in a quiet moment, but not so fine if it is something you know you will regret later.

So how can you use focus to gain control? Focus on your goals, your dreams, your visions. Focus on the rewards you will reap when you make them happen. Focus on the pain you will experience if you do not take the right steps or achieve your goals. Focus on feeling good. Focus on knowing you are a 10. Focus on the beauty and wonder of life. Focus on the opportunities you have. Focus on the possibilities. Focus on your ability to focus. It is the key; it is the first step that can get momentum working for you or against you.

What can you do to keep this incredible concept on the front burner? Program your environment so that it helps you to focus on the right things. Put up signs and reminders everywhere, e.g., "Focus!" Affirm day in and day out, "I can control what I focus on."

Remember, your focus is your gatekeeper; it is the start of anything good or great, or, conversely, anything bad or perverse. It is the movie screen of your mind that presents life-enhancing opportunities or time-wasting, go-nowhere destructive behaviors. It is the first step that flows out of your ability to choose; it presents to your mind what to consider. What you pay attention to has consequences. If you pay attention to the horrors, the suffering, the lack, the cruelty, the obscenities committed by people against one another, these considerations will flood you with bad feelings. If you focus on the hurts others have inflicted on you, it will conjure up feelings of anger. If you focus on all your mistakes or your immoral acts, it will unleash feelings of guilt, self-hatred, and loathing. If you focus on the catastrophes of tomorrow, it will flood your spirit with worry and anxiety. If you focus on the faults of others, their mistakes, their defects, you will hold them in contempt, and very likely follow it up with criticism. If you focus on your own lacks and compare them with those folks who have it all, you will feel inferior.

Your focus leads to feelings. If you want to feel good all the time, then it is simple: Focus on the things that bring on good feelings. Think of yourself in possession of some goal you want badly to achieve, e.g., a new car. See yourself in it, driving it, smell the leather, hear the quiet throaty roar of the engine, and notice how you feel. A smile comes to your face, and voilà—you feel good. What is the business you're in—feeling good or feeling bad?

Summary and Bridge

This chapter deals with your most unique human power: your power to choose. It explores the question of why people behave the way they do, and the source of all motivation, pleasure and avoiding pain. It discusses strategies for using and amplifying these concepts for a grander life. It also discusses the gatekeeping role focus plays and emphasizes, "You can control what you focus on."

The next chapter extends the discussion of choice to the moral dimension and suggests criteria to apply that can keep you on the side of the angels in selling and in life.

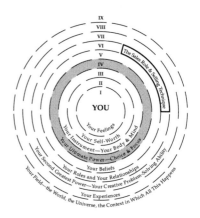

9

The Ethical Salesperson: The Only Way to Go

	Yes	No
1. Is it important for you to have repeat business?	☐	☐
2. Do you ever have ambiguity in your mind as to what is the right thing to do?	☐	☐
3. Would you like to have criteria at your fingertips that could help you through the moral mazes?	☐	☐

In my judgment, the best way to get a customer is to get the customer for life. There is a temptation in so many quarters to get the sale now—don't worry about tomorrow. This is related to the short-term-itis that afflicts American business in general. What this does is to put pressures on salespeople that may be so strong that there is a temptation to cheat. When this is overlaid with greed for more, which is embraced by many salespeople, it is no wonder that selling, sales, and salesmanship are associated with snake oil, conning, sleight of hand, bait and switch, the "do I have a deal for you" pitch, and promises, promises with no delivery on them. If, after a sale, you get in your wagon, move on to the next town, and never see the customer again, you don't have to worry about customer satisfaction. But if you are involved in a competitive marketplace and want to build a business that will last forever and have repeat business, referrals, and customers for a lifetime, then the only way to go is to be honest, ethical, and trusting—a man or woman of your word.

The payoff for acting in an ethical manner is that the customer trusts you. Trust is the firmest foundation on which to build a relationship. But it comes only from acting in an honorable way. If the customer concludes that you have acted in a less than honorable way, then you can be assured that if a sale does occur, it will be a one-sale relationship. The fact is, it is tougher to do business when you are dishonorable. Why? Reputation. A customer's bad experience does not occur in a vacuum. That customer will send out bad, negative, hurtful ripples throughout his or her world of relationships, and in no time your reputation is drowning in bad publicity.

One way to get beyond the short-term-itis and realize the incredible value of a customer, and this is simply from a dollars-and-cents viewpoint, is to estimate what amount of business could possibly come from this customer over a ten-year period. Further, just as customer dissatisfaction will send out negative ripples, customer satisfaction will send out positive ripples, and from such positive ripples referrals come. A conservative estimate is that over a ten-year period, from one satisfied customer you are likely to get at least two referrals who will give you an amount of business comparable to that of the satisfied customer. So look at the arithmetic. Suppose you sold a car to a customer for $20,000. Suppose the customer was thrilled with your service. Over a ten-year period, it is likely that the customer will buy two more cars from you, totaling $40,000. Thus the ten-year value of the initial sale is $60,000. If that customer refers two buyers like himself to you, whom you also satisfy, that means the ten-year value of their sales is $120,000. Thus, if you total the value of the initial sale in terms of its potential, it comes to $180,000.

All a salesperson has to do to destroy this positive rippling effect is to do something unethical or dishonorable—the ripples will occur in reverse. However, the right thing to do is not always clear. What is the correct moral choice to make in a given situation? One set of guidelines you can use to help you think through a moral maze is the ethics check. The questions will help you determine what is an ethical position for yourself. They were originally introduced in Ken Blanchard and Norman Vincent Peale's book, *The Power of Ethical Management*; I have applied them to selling.

1. *Does the action or intended action violate any civil law or company policy?* If the answer to this question is yes, on either civil law or company policy, don't do it. If you do it anyway, you are exposing yourself to a very high risk that could come back to haunt you. If your customer is aware of the violations and wants you to do it anyway, you are not dealing with an honorable customer. And if the customer is aware of these violations, you will certainly not go up in his or her esteem—just the reverse. You will be seen as an opportunist who is willing to shave ethical corners. In my judgment, from both an ethical and a pragmatic viewpoint, the wiser course is to keep all your actions in conformity with civil law and your company policy.

2. *Is it fair to all concerned?* Justice, fairness, and equity have to be at the base of any decent contract. Suppose you sell a buyer a house that the buyer thinks is a three-family house, but that in fact is legally two-family, and you do not advise him or her of that fact. The buyer's investment can be in jeopardy if a housing inspector forbids three-family occupancy. It is not sufficient to adopt the "buyer beware" posture and maintain that it is up to the buyer to find any defects in the product or service. I think the ethical thing to do is to keep the playing field level and, as the seller, supply all the appropriate information that would ground a sale in justice. Just as you would want to be treated fairly in any transaction, so, to follow the Golden Rule, it makes sense to treat others fairly. Furthermore, if a customer has a distinct sense that you have treated him or her unfairly, you can bet that you will get no more business ever from that person, and that he or she will tell anyone he or she knows what a bad deal you gave. In other words, an unfair transaction in which you are the beneficiary will guarantee a one-sale relationship.

3. *Does the action, real or intended, make me feel proud?* There are a number of tests that can let you know whether you are proud of something. Ask yourself, "How would my mother feel about my behavior, if she knew it?" Would she smile in approval and want to tell everybody, or would she want to hide because of the embarrassment you caused? This fantasy will put you in touch with the ethics you were brought up with as a child.

Another fantasy to run by your mind is this: Suppose what you did was emblazoned across your local newspaper in two-inch headlines. How would you feel? How would your spouse, your children, your friends, your parents, your community feel? Would you be running for cover? Loading up the moving van to get out of town? Or would you be walking down Main Street with your head up high? While you are reflecting on the moral choices involved, you can always do the "mirror test." Look into your eyes as you stare into a mirror, and ask yourself, "Is this the right thing to do?"

If in Doubt

If you are in doubt about what to do, my advice is to err by being on the side of the angels. If you are puzzled as to where that side might be, it is a good idea to seek out a person who is known for his or her character, who routinely models honorable behavior, and ask that person's advice.

Another strategy is to do an MRE, and when you are in a state of deep relaxation, imagine that sitting around a table are three people whom you respect for their upright character. These folks can be alive or dead. In your fantasy, tell them that you have a problem you are working on, what it is, and that you would like their advice. Observe what each says, listen to their arguments back and forth, and then synthesize their message. Finally, open your eyes and write it down. This message represents your inner voice, and is a message it would be wise to consider seriously.

Acting ethically is a good policy. It is the right thing to do. It is also good business. As mentioned, any enduring relationship is built on trust. What is trust? It is a state of mind a person holds, an expectation vis-à-vis another that the other person is honest, caring, reliable, consistent, and fair, and will act in such a manner. When trust occurs in a relationship, it is the equivalent of an open door. The customer feels that you will not hurt him or her in any way, that you have his or her interests at heart. He or she is not worried, paranoic, or fearful of getting the short end of the stick.

Other Considerations

Sometimes you are puzzled as to the correct course of action, and you do the ethics check, yet you are not comfortable with the decision. It is important to know that many times, when you act ethically, you will not like it. You may even feel sorry that you have to do the right thing, and doing the right thing may even put you in jeopardy. It is not by chance that our Congress has enacted a whistleblower law designed to protect those who stand up to fraud and corruption. Historically, and even despite the law, the fate of whistleblowers, or people who choose to act ethically, is well known. They are virtually guaranteed to be stigmatized, receive all kinds of punishment, and have opprobrium heaped on them. It is not always popular to be on the side of the angels.

One way to acquire greater intellectual support for a course of action is to ask yourself, "What is for the greater good of the organization?" Suppose you are a sales manager and you have a problem concerning the poor performance of an employee, a long-time friend who has been in a tailspin for two years. You know the man's family, you have drunk many a beer together, yet you know he has to go. If you make your decision based on what is in the interests of the greater good of the company, you can terminate the person with a clear conscience. Clearly, whistleblowers, when they do indict members of their own company for corruption, are not doing it to destroy their company; rather, in the long term it is in the best interest of the company to behave in a legal and ethical manner. Likewise, if a salesperson is approached by a customer for a bribe, in the short run it would get an order, but in the long term the greater good of the company could be compromised profoundly.

The reason why the greater good of the company is so important is that the selfish interests of one person can compromise the mission of the company, and in extreme cases of personal greed, corruption, or fraud, whole companies have been known to go down in flames because of the venality of one person. This important point is enshrined in the principle of eminent domain, which is used all the time by communities, cities, and states that engineer improvements in roads, water flow, piping, or electrical lines, for example, that may disadvantage one individual, but bring benefit to the society.

Summary and Bridge

A yes! to ethical behavior in selling is not only the right thing to do, it is good business. Although it is tough to be on the side of the angels at times, in the long run it will benefit your company's reputation, and your reputation. The positive ripples will go far beyond the present transaction you might be involved in. The ethics check and considering what is in the best interests of your company, the greater good of the most people, are helpful criteria to orient your ethical compass.

The next chapter puts everything that has been discussed so far in the context of your belief system.

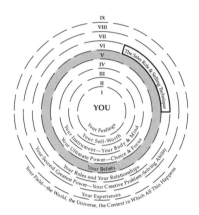

10

Core Beliefs That Emancipate

	Yes	No
1. Do you want to know the core belief that is the ultimate empowerment?	☐	☐
2. Would you like to learn the core belief about others that lays the foundation for a solid relationship?	☐	☐
3. Would you like to learn how to transform the negative associations of your occupation that you have?	☐	☐

There is a stark fact that will send profound ripples through everything you do and experience, and it is this: What you believe is your reality. The meaning that you attach to something is your reality. As you believe, so it is. Believe it, and you will see it. What is a belief? It is a subjective assent to a truth that a person perceives. A belief is a statement about what something is—what something means. A belief, in fact, is a judgment, and it has two key dimensions: Something is either true or false; something is either good or bad.

So, when I say to you, "You are a 10," I believe that what I am saying is true about you, and further, that it is good for you to believe that about yourself. The fact is, you have to believe something about yourself, and either you can believe what others have told you about yourself, or you can decide, *choose*, to see yourself in a life-enhancing manner. And this last thought is either going to be the springboard to your liberation and the key to unlock any chains that might hold you down or inhibit you, or going to slam shut the prison door of pain and misery. To be more emphatic: You can choose what you want to believe about yourself, or about anything.

The incredible thing about the statement above is that if you believe you do not have that power, you are right—you don't. If you think you can't choose to believe what you want to about yourself, you won't ever exercise that choice. The choice is yours to make, but if you believe you have no choice, you will never choose something better. So, the ultimate core belief that is going to send energizing waves throughout your life is a belief in your power to change, your power to choose, your power to decide to be something more and to do something greater with your life and talent. On the other hand, the belief that will suck you into a quagmire of negativity and fatalism is the conviction—the belief—that you are powerless, that you can't change, that there is nothing you can do about much of anything. Whereas the former conviction about your personal ability to choose your beliefs is the greatest empowerment you can have, and one that you give to yourself, the affirmation of that *inability* is the ultimate self-disenfranchisement, the key to a life of victimization and powerlessness.

What Other Core Beliefs Are There?

Another core belief that affects all your relationships is what you hold to be true about others. Others can be defined as predators, people whom you can't trust or who will hurt you. The result of this mindset is that you keep others at a distance. You perceive others as a threat that you have to control if you are going to have a relationship with them. Believers in this perspective have few, if any, friends or lovers, and rarely experience intimacy. What they have are relationships with others in which they have to do it first, before others do it to them. Salespeople who have this core belief extend it to customers and coworkers. They really hate these others and are always waiting to get the short end of the stick from them. They believe that everyone is into lying, cheating, deceit, and selfish behavior. As a consequence, selling is not much fun for them, even if they do make their numbers.

What is a core belief about others that is not Pollyannaish, but is consistent with your own sense of 10ness? It is this: Other people are 10s, too. What this implies is that your orientation to others is open, based on the wish, desire, hope, and expectation that the other people will be kind and honest in their behavior. Most of the time, what you expect, you will get. But what do you do if someone behaves in an unethical, hurtful, criminal manner? Do you just stand there and turn the other cheek, because they are 10s, albeit misguided? Absolutely not. As much as I am for kindness, love, trust, and honesty as an operating disposition toward others, there are sharks out there who are trying to nail you. In that case, seek justice, be assertive, and if possible make them suffer the consequences of their deviance.

How do you apply this to selling? Well, understand that your prospects, or customers, are 10s, but even more important, they have a burning need to feel like 10s. That's where your behavior, your thoughtfulness, and your listening ability come in. When you think about your customers this way, and plan in advance how you can help them feel special, you will discover that it will be reciprocated with great frequency, and will create an environment for selling that is friendly, easy, and successful.

Core Beliefs About Selling

The fundamental choice you have to make is whether you want to govern your life by beliefs that are dumb, destructive, harmful, and irrational, or whether you want to govern your life and your interpretation of it by reasonable, life-enhancing beliefs. Let's say, for the sake of discussion, that you want to choose beliefs that are reasonable and life-enhancing.

Well, let's take a look at the meanings people associate with key words in your occupation. Take the word *salesman*. What are the associations most folks have? If you are not sure, ask them, but this is what they are likely to associate with the word: snake oil, pushy, sharpie, con artist, a beggar, untrustworthy, greedy, money mad, and an irritation, annoyance, and intrusion. Now whether you are aware of it or not, you have internalized these same connotations attached to the word *salesman*. If you have not consciously transformed the meanings you have attached to the word, and you are in fact a salesperson, is it any wonder that you are ashamed or embarrassed to let anyone know what you do, and that you feel inferior to most folks you approach (especially customers)?

Remember what I said earlier: "What you believe is your reality." So transform your own meaning of what a salesperson is. How? Think of a salesperson as one who presents opportunity to others. That opportunity is either a product or a service that can help a customer fill a need. Think of yourself as a helper, as a partner, as a friend who wants to improve the life of your customer. Think of yourself as a problem solver: You have a solution to a customer's problem, and you are anxious to present the solution to him or her. You see, what you have with these meanings is an altruistic, sensitive, other-oriented interpretation of what selling is all about.

The kind of behavior that flows out of this perspective is analogous to that of a missionary who has the "good news" and is thrilled to have the opportunity to present it to anyone who will listen. A salesperson with these meanings of the task is bold, fearless, and selfless, and truly believes his or her calling is to improve the life of the customer. There is no inferiority here. There is no hatred of the customer. There is no reluctance to take the steps that will create a situation in which you can present the good news.

Think about this metaphor of you as a missionary on fire with your good news. Your metaphors will influence your behavior profoundly. If you see the customer as the enemy, then you must attack the situation, overcome the obstacles, get intelligence, decimate the competition, and bring back a "coup"—it will support feelings that are hostile, and behavior that is ruthless. A salesperson as missionary is a vastly more benign metaphor, and implies a bright fire of enthusiasm about the product or service that will get captured in the salesperson's presentation of himself or herself.

If you define the customer as a person in need, he or she needs your good news. The customer is in trouble. Sometimes customers don't realize this, and it is your duty to help them realize it. But a customer, just by his or her presence, is asking for help. When you look at the customer this way, you are no longer intimidated, you are no longer in a one-down position. You are in fact doing the customer a favor; you are there to help, to give him or her the good news that can help solve an important problem. Now the process of selling is no longer simply one of overcoming objections, but of showing the customer how the need that he or she has revealed can be satisfactorily filled by your good news. We are talking about persuasion, but you will never persuade anyone about anything if you don't believe it yourself. This is where the feeling element comes into your good news. You believe it; you are excited about it; you are convinced it is the best solution to the customer's problem.

Customers love to buy from people who exude a belief, a conviction, an assurance, and a confidence in what they recommend.

Other Metaphors

There are any number of other metaphors you can use to purge the negativity associated with selling. For example, think of yourself as a doctor. A doctor is in an altruistic profession that receives the respect of others. A doctor relieves pain and restores health to a diseased body. You are a sales doctor. You diagnose the customer's illness and recommend a remedy that will make the customer whole.

Think of yourself as a consultant. What does a consultant do? A consultant analyzes a situation, collects information, and, based on the analysis, makes a recommendation for improvement.

Think of yourself as a problem solver. You deal in solutions. You help the customer define the problem, entertain possible solutions, and then propose one that makes sense.

In every one of these cases, the customer will feel better and be more effective, integrated, and functional. You have served; you have helped; you have done good. The payoff and the commission are simply an effect; the driving force here is the altruistic, ethical, and noble behavior.

Other Core Beliefs

The key to great selling is making large numbers of sales calls. However, "call reluctance" is one of the occupational conditions that many in outside sales experience. Call reluctance refers to the inhibition that enchains a salesperson, preventing him or her from making the kind and quantity of sales calls that make good sense. Call reluctance results in opportunity lost, time wasted, and fewer sales. It also engenders a profound guilt in the salesperson who is into avoidance activity. This guilt drives many out of the profession, and drives those that stay into the use of pain killers like drugs, alcohol, and smoking, to name a few.

Since everyone knows that selling is a numbers game, meaning that the more prospects you contact, the more sales you will get, it is worth exploring some of the reasons for a salesperson's reluctance to call. I think many of the impediments to courage, fearlessness, and ability to call operate on a level below conscious awareness. But all of them are in the mind and have to do with avoiding pain. (Aspects of this were discussed earlier with reference to choice.) The pain is what the salesperson experiences when he or she violates a standard of behavior that has been internalized. When these standards that support call reluctance are held up to scrutiny, most are seen to be irrational. If the salesperson realized that they were irrational and replaced them with reasonable ones, the intellectual support for call reluctance would evaporate. Let's look at some of these standards, which, incidentally, come from parents or significant others when a person is in the early formative years. Notice the absolute character of the standards:

- Don't impose on other people.
- If you want something done, do it yourself.
- Don't talk to strangers.
- You should always be liked by everyone.
- Don't make others uncomfortable.
- Don't ask others embarrassing questions.

- Don't do anything that would make you disliked by others.
- Don't ask others for help.
- Don't ask.
- What others think or say is more important than what you think or say.
- Other people are better than you—are in a higher position, have more education, have more income, etc.
- People in high positions should never be interrupted by the likes of you.
- Avoid pain at all costs.
- Don't put yourself in a position to be rejected.
- Don't ever fail.

If a salesperson has internalized any one of these standards, it can be difficult for him or her to do what needs to be done to make sales. Why? Because in the act of cold calling for appointments or making sales calls, the salesperson is violating the standard. Whenever a standard is violated, it will engender guilt in the violator, i.e., he or she is a "bad boy" or "bad girl." Since one of the great motivating forces for a person is to avoid pain, many salespeople will avoid the pain, or the guilt, by not making the calls. By solving the problem of guilt, they create another problem: they do not make sales. This causes underperformance, great stress, and often greater pain and more guilt.

The Big Question

The big question is, therefore, how can a person be absolutely fearless, and in fact enthusiastic, about making appointments and sales calls? Let's go back to the ultimate core belief, "As you define it, so it is." Remember, you have the power to define your own core beliefs and your own standards, because it is your life, and you are responsible for making yourself happy or miserable—*no one else is.*

So what kinds of standards could, in fact, motivate you to fearlessness in making calls?

- You should help others, and what you are offering does that.
- You should ask of anyone anything you need to help the sale.

- You should give them (prospects) permission not to be helped by you today.
- You should realize that there is no man or woman on this planet better than you—you are a 10; conversely, there is no one inferior to you either—they are 10s also, but 10s in need of what you have to offer.

These standards can replace the unreasonable ones noted earlier, and I exhort you to embrace them. To support that process, be a good parent to yourself and give yourself the following permission. It is a permission that allows you to be proactive in every aspect of selling. This is the key permission: In everything that is legal and ethical, it is OK to ask anyone anything. It is the key that gives you the information you need, and the key to closing.

Give yourself this permission, embrace the reasonable standards, and one of the great obstacles to your achievement is eliminated. You may already have done this; in that event, this will help you understand what is behind some of the difficulties your low-performing brethren have.

Summary and Bridge

The ultimate core belief is that you have the power to choose what you want to believe. You can control what you want to believe about anything. The 10s of the world choose to govern their lives by reasonable, life-enhancing beliefs. When you apply these concepts to the occupation of selling, you have a way to transform the meanings that you, and certainly others, may have attached to words like *selling, salesman, customer*. The new beliefs suggested are life-enhancing and energizing, and make the embracer of them fearless and courageous in sharing his or her good news. Also, by giving yourself permission to ask anything that is legal and ethical, you have a belief springboard that banishes call reluctance and leads to great sales.

As you proceed to adopt these kinds of beliefs, you will experience the positive ripples generated by yeses in the arenas mentioned, and you will see that they do amplify energy and good feelings. The next chapter continues this discussion of obstacles to sales and how to remove them.

11

The Salesperson's Four Greatest Nemeses

	Yes	No
1. Is it useful to know some of the great obstacles that stand in the way of star performance?	☐	☐
2. Would you like to learn how to unshackle yourself from inhibition and become more bold and courageous?	☐	☐
3. Would you like to experience the "incredible lightness of being"?	☐	☐

Fear

What is fear? What consequences can it have for a salesperson? Who experiences it? When does it occur? How does it get stimulated? Why does one person have it and another person not? If you do experience it, how can you overcome it? First of all, fear is a multidimensional phenomenon. How does fear begin? It begins with a perception. The perception is interpreted, which is to say, a meaning is attached to it. The meaning immediately gets alloyed to a condemning judgment—it is bad, dangerous, hurtful, harmful, and injurious. The judgment floods the person with feelings of dread and fright; that which is the object of the fear is to be avoided. In the first instance, fears are taught by others in our culture, or the object of fear in the present may have inflicted some harm on the perceiver in the past, and the person remembers it. So, for example, if a woman has been taught to be afraid of snakes or has had a bad experience in the past with a snake, and, lo and behold, a snake crosses her path as she is walking along, she perceives and sees the snake as a threat—something bad and harmful. Feelings of fright erupt, and the wish to avoid the danger and flee occurs.

Now that's the process, but it is important to realize that fear is not in itself bad. In fact, in the face of real threats, it is a desirable emotion and can have a lot to do with a person's survival. What is necessary is to take a look at the object that precipitates the fear and analyze whether it is, in fact, a real threat or an imagined one, and therefore rooted in irrationality.

Take, for example, a salesperson who is afraid to make a cold call. Most of the presumed threat does not stand up under scrutiny. (Most salespeople, incidentally, will deny that they are afraid to make cold calls, even if they really are.) But if you could put it in words, the salesperson is afraid of being ridiculed, of being embarrassed, of being criticized, or of being denigrated. What does the salesperson who is afraid to make sales calls focus on? The pain, the discomfort, the hurt that he or she believes will come. He or she knows it is bad; this unleashes the dread, and avoidance behavior occurs. Remember, the great motivating force that explains a lot of behavior is the profound need to avoid pain. The whole scene of cold calling is defined in full, luxuriant pain, psychological, sociological, and physiological, and then it is catastrophized to such an extent that cold calling becomes an awful thing to be avoided at all costs. What is the consequence? The salesperson does not do it, and an opportunity to create a sale is lost.

I have no objections to reasonable fears, but unreasonable fears need to be met head on, and the threats seen for what they are—

harmless or, if harmful at all, minuscule in the degree of pain that is experienced. Psychologists tell us that the best way to deal with irrational fears is to do the very thing we fear. Once we do it, the very doing of it demonstrates that the pains we expected were all in the mind, and did not in fact occur. A few repetitions of the thing feared, and the fears gradually evaporate. As I mentioned in the preface, in my early career as a salesman, when I had no connections and no referrals, I started out with a blank slate. I had seminars I wanted to sell, which I believed addressed felt needs in organizations. I developed a prospect list with hundreds of names on it, but nobody knew about me, and I had to start the process of getting in front of prospects, so I had to make appointments with them. I would sit down at my desk and plan on making twenty phone calls. Initially, when I started this process, I found it painful, and I would play mind games with myself to avoid the task, like reading *The Wall Street Journal* and *The New York Times*, doing paperwork, or dialing the weather just to get some of my quota in. But I did most of it, and I discovered that a prospect could not crawl through the phone and strangle me or hurt me. In fact, 99.9 percent of the time I was treated with the utmost courtesy. After a while, what happened? I got appointments, and with appointments I got the opportunity to give presentations, and eventually close sales. By acting against the fear, I got so good at cold calling and making appointments that I eventually taught others how to do it.

However, to this day, I remember the time I had my first in-person call with a superintendent of schools. I had practiced and rehearsed my sales interview, built around the concepts of interest, money and decision, and effective questioning, to get me where I wanted to go. On the morning of the appointment, I called in advance to confirm it, hoping against hope that he had cancelled it. But he hadn't. I was filled with fear and trembling, but I entered the office, did what I had prepared and, to make a long story short, got him to convene a panel of administrators for the following week. I came back and gave them a presentation; immediately afterward they voted yes, and I got my first two thousand dollar contract—I could hardly believe it had happened.

Did I experience fear here? Yes, in making the appointment, in doing the interview, and in presenting to the administrators. What was the fear? Not only was I afraid I would fail, but I was even afraid I would succeed. Was the fear reasonable? Yes. There was a possibility that I could screw up royally. But what did I do? I prepared, rehearsed, and prepared some more, but I did the thing I feared, and I succeeded. Since 1974, I have become fearless, in cold calling, in interviews, in presentations, in closing, and, of course, in delivering quality service. I say this not to pat myself on the back, but to remind any one of you that most of the fears you have are of no account, and that by doing the right things and going against them, they are banished permanently.

The Best Way to Act Against Your Irrational Fears

It is not the reasonable fears that are to be ignored. Knowledge, skill, preparation, planning, and doing the thing feared are the way to approach them. What about the other fears? Well, suppose you have done a reward-cost analysis, and have determined that doing something can have significant positive payoffs, yet you are are scared, reluctant, and fearful about taking the steps to make it happen. How can you give yourself a reality check? Ask yourself two questions, which, incidentally, I got from Robert Ringer, who—despite a rather odious philosophy—made a real contribution with them.

1. What is the worst thing that can happen if I do it?
2. If that indeed happened, could I live with it?

If the answer to the second question is no, then don't do it. If the answer to the second question is yes, and the possibility of significant reward exists, do it.

Let us suppose that you are terrified at the thought of speaking in public, and that heretofore you have avoided putting yourself in that position because you know you will fail. Let's suppose, further, that in your new sales position you will be required to give stand-up presentations to groups of people, and you are wondering whether you should take the position or not. The first question is, What is the worst thing that could happen if you did take the position? Well, you could give a presentation and forget what you were saying, or give a poor presentation and not get the sale. The second question is, Could you live with that possible outcome? The answer is clearly yes. You would still be alive; you would not be fired; you would still have more opportunities with other customers to get it right. So, the answer is to do it. The strategy for success is straightforward: prepare, prepare, rehearse, rehearse, rehearse, and then do it.

How Not to Fail at Anything

One of the great fears salespeople have is the fear of failure—the fear that they will become a loser, a waste product, someone who can't make it, a permanent strikeout. Let's examine what failure is. Failure is an outcome. It is an effect. It is a result. It is a conclusion. It is a condemning judgment that someone, or something, has not met an acceptable standard of performance. Part of the pain associated with failing comes from what I call the dumb Vince Lombardi philosophy of life, "Winning isn't everything, it's the only thing." This means that if you are not *number one,* you did not win, and therefore you are a loser—a failure. If you believe this, you are in deep trouble, because no matter what you do, there is only one winner and many losers—just from a statistical viewpoint, most people are consigned to the scrap heap if they believe this nonsense. People who do believe this do one of three things: They win (rare), they lose and are miserable a lot, or they don't even enter the race and try.

In life there are few sure things. There are few things that are guaranteed. In fact, just the opposite is the case. Uncertainty abounds; outcomes of actions always have probabilities of success. What a probability means is that there is some chance of error, of failure. If all a person does in life is "the almost sure thing," it virtually guarantees that he or she will not grow very much. Why? Because in order to grow, we have to venture out into the unknown; we have to take a risk. But if a failure is a catastrophe, and if a person generalizes a failing experience and concludes therefore that "I am a failure," that person will either not take many risks, and therefore will not grow very much, or, if the person does take a risk and fails, is likely to define himself or herself as a failure. In either event, the propensity to take a risk is low. People of this kind are rarely salespeople, and if they are, they are right up there with the most troubled people in the profession.

Now to answer the question, "What can you do to *never* fail at anything?" The answer is to change your standard of acceptable performance. The standard of acceptable performance that makes sense to me is the following: The only time I can fail at something is when I do not learn anything from the experience.

Why is this interpretation of failure so radical, refreshing, and motivating? Because, when you do not hit a quota, target, or goal, it does not become an opportunity for self-indictment, self-condemnation, or being miserable. Rather, it becomes an opportunity to learn something about what you just did—what went wrong; how you could do it better or differently. When you define risk taking this way, it emboldens you to meet fears head on. After a reward/cost analysis, if a course of action makes sense, the worst thing that can happen is that you might learn something. This concept is powerful because if you believe it, you can literally fail your way to success. How? You try something; it doesn't work; you say, "What can I learn about what I just did?" You pull a lesson learned out of it; now you are smarter, more experienced, wiser. You then try something new and different and better, and you will eventually discover something that works. The beauty of this approach is that there is less agita, less stress, less pain; the approach is filled with hope and a sense of positive expectation. And then what happens? You will feel better, and that will put you into an achieving state. Then you get on with it. That's how folks grow.

A Second Great Nemesis: Rejection

Most people want to be loved, accepted, valued, and appreciated. Most people do not like it when they are rejected by another; and since so many people have identified their self-worth with their ideas, work, product, or creative expressions, when you reject those things, you are really rejecting them. A lot of the pain associated with rejection has to do with buying the nonsense I refuted in the chapter on self-worth. Many people, nevertheless, make that identification, and in effect, when they call on you, ask you to buy, or ask you to listen to their story or to accept their proposal, they are not giving you permission to say no. They are holding an absolutist expectation, and it gets packaged in the form of a *should,* "You should give me an appointment; you should buy my product; you should listen to me; you should accept my proposal." In their mind they are not allowing you to say no. What happens when you do say no? Well, they get upset and, in particular, angry, because you shouldn't reject them; you're not allowed to; you're not supposed to. Often this anger then gets directed inward, and they second-guess themselves, their own worth, and their own value.

So, step one in handling rejection is to remember the essence of your 10ness. You are not your work, or your product, or your idea. You are a 10; that is a constant; that is an absolute; that is one concept that need never change. It is your anchor and your bulwark against the rejection, criticism, or attacks of others. Your 10ness does not depend on whether someone accepts your idea, your product, your proposal.

How else can you deal with a rejection? Just as in taking a risk and looking for a lesson learned when a failing experience occurs, you can convert a rejection into an opportunity to learn something. All you have to do when you are rejected is to ask why. The answer to that question is something you can register that will make you a little smarter and a little wiser. So once again, if you look on rejection as an opportunity to learn something, you neutralize a great deal of the pain, you do not get caught up in manipulative absolutism in your expectations, and you are not blown out of the water when it happens. I say *when* it happens because there is no way I know of that anyone can go through life without being rejected by someone else for something. So, keep the "lessons learned" model on the front burner.

Another way to ease the pain of a rejection is to consider the rejector. Where is the rejector coming from? What problems does the rejector have? What are the alternatives the rejector has been considering? What is his or her motivation for giving you a rejection? Is it possible that your rejection has nothing to do with you? Where do you think you are on the list of priorities of the rejector? This empathetic analysis can generate some new insight, and help you realize that there may be a myriad of other factors at work that have little to do with the quality of your idea, your work, your product, or your proposal.

Perspective

Often folks make themselves miserable by fixating on their pain, their sense of victimization, what a bad deal they have gotten. Remember, what you focus on will be your experience. One way to unfocus the laser beam of pain is to put the rejection in perspective. How? Do these four things. First, reflect on this rejection, and see how it compares to all the things in your life that you have suffered through and yet managed to survive and grow. Second, if you are brave, in your mind's eye, put yourself on your deathbed, and from that vantage point reflect on how this rejection looks in the perspective of your entire life. Third, compare the pain you are experiencing right now with that of the refugees from Haiti, Rwanda, or Bosnia; do a quick scan of the sad cases in your local hospital; listen to the latest horror on the six o'clock news; think of the tornadoes, the hurricanes, and the earthquakes that have recently happened. Think how any of these folks would give their eyeteeth to have your rejection in exchange for their problem. And fourth, if you have an evolutionary view of the world, think about the suffering, deaths, diseases, plagues, cataclysms, wars, torturings, holocausts, and racial, ethnic, and tribal cleansings that have occurred since the beginning of history. Once again, compare them to your rejection. This analysis is what I call the "pain shrinker." The beauty of it is that it de-emotionalizes your rejection, and readily puts you into a problem-solving mode where you are in a position to say, "What can I do about my problem?"

Fall in Love With a No

Another powerful way to make you impervious to a no is to change what the meaning of a no is for you. If in the past a no hurt, was a pain, engendered disappointment, and put your fire out, and you hated it when you got one, then you are indeed a candidate for relief. How can you redefine a no?

Let me tell you how I did it. First of all, I examined the numbers that my sell cycle generated, and this is something you can also do. I mentioned earlier that I would make twenty phone calls to get appointments. Typically, the twenty calls would get me two appointments. Of the two appointments, I would get one invitation to come back and give a presentation. When I gave a presentation, I would typically close at a 99 percent rate. In my early years of selling, the typical value of a seminar sold was $2,000. Now think about the twenty phone calls that I made. On average, I had to get eighteen noes or not-ins to get two appointments, or nine noes or not-ins for one appointment. The way I fell in love with a no was by defining each no as forward progress—each no I got was getting me closer to a yes. I knew I had to get nine noes to get a yes, so I would just sit down expecting nine noes, and as I was getting my quota of noes I often got surprised—sometimes I would get an appointment after only the third call!

Selling is a numbers game. Once you know your numbers, you know how much progress each no constitutes. I used to go one step further and divide the twenty calls into the end result of my calls, namely, $2,000, and calculate that each call was worth $100. So I would make a call, get a no, make another call, get another no, and step back and say out loud, "Damn, I just made two hundred bucks!"

Do your numbers, and test it out. We all have a success ratio.

The Ever-Renewing Market

Just because you have been rejected by a customer today does not necessarily mean you will be rejected tomorrow because the market universe in which you operate is changing every three years. At any given point in time, a number of things are happening. Some of your prospects are getting promoted; some die; some leave their present company and go to another; some have been badly disappointed by their present vendor; some are actively looking for you, only you don't know about it; some have mellowed in their old age; some know someone else who needs your product or service; some are growing and need a second source; some realize that price is not the chief criterion; some are waiting for you to call. The problem with this is that in your universe of prospects, these events are occurring randomly. But what you do know is that your marketplace is renewing itself at least every three years.

How do you deal with this? Always leave your door open when you are dealing with a prospect or a customer. Always stay in touch. Always come back. Always ask, "Is today the day?" And incredibly, eventually it will be.

The Third and Fourth Great Nemeses

Guilt and anger are the other two nemeses that can profoundly inhibit a salesperson from being all that he or she could be. They can be treated together because there are similarities in the process that causes them and similarities in the way to deal with them.

First, let us start off with an assertion that there is good guilt and righteous anger, and that there is nothing wrong with these emotions. There is, however, excessive guilt, irrational guilt, and chronic unspecific guilt that it makes sense to jettison. There is anger that is ill-founded and excessive, and it, likewise, should be given the eject button if you really want to be happy and to experience what it's like to be a free spirit.

Let's understand the process in terms of how guilt and anger occur. Once you do this, what you need to do to let guilt and anger go will become apparent. The process starts with a measuring stick. The measuring stick is in your mind, and it is the *standard* you apply to a behavior. Where do the standards come from? From your mother and father, teachers, preachers, the media, or others; you might even have invented them yourself. Regardless of the source, you have them, and you use them as the benchmark, as the ruler, as the standard against which you compare your own or someone else's behavior. These standards are thought about linguistically in terms of *shoulds*—for example, I should not kill you; you should not lie to me; you should be honest; I should not make mistakes.

Now let's take a look at an "I should" and dissect how guilt emanates from the process. Here is the standard: "I should always tell the truth." On a given day, an occasion arises where you find that you are lying, but you continue lying anyway. Afterward, when you reflect on your standard of truthfulness and recall that you did lie, you make a condemning judgment. This self-condemning judgment can come out in a variety of expressions, such as "What's the matter with me!"; "I was wrong to have done that"; "I should not have done that (bad, dishonest, awful, spineless, sinful) thing." Such expressions have a moral dimension—something is good or it's bad, and in this instance your behavior is bad. Once the self-condemning moral judgment of your badness is made, you get flooded with guilt. Now, that's the process whenever you experience guilt.

Let's take a look at anger. The process is similar. You have a standard, a should, that you apply to someone else's behavior, e.g., "You should always tell the truth to me." Suppose that someone is your spouse, and your spouse lies to you about an expenditure. You observe the discrepancy between your standard and your spouse's behavior, and you follow that with a condemning judgment which, once again, can take many forms, all of which have a moral connotation: "What's the matter with you!"; "You shouldn't have lied to me"; "You were (wrong, bad, dishonest, unethical, devious, calculating, untrustworthy) to have lied." When the condemning judgment is made, it unleashes the feelings of anger. The judgment is the gate opener to the strong feelings.

In both guilt and anger, the process is the same: a should that is violated, a condemning judgment, and the feeling. Although guilt and anger are bona fide human emotions and ought to be expressed appropriately, once they have been expressed, the wiser course is to get on with life and stop harboring the feelings. Why? Because the amount of personal energy it takes to support the feelings of anger and guilt is enormous. The more of your energy that is invested in these feelings, the less you have left over for good feelings; getting into an achieving state; solving problems; expressing yourself creatively; having fun, laughter, affection, and intimacy with someone you care for; or, to bring you back to your occupation, selling effectively.

Okay, how can you put it behind you? How can you let it go? There are two strategies that I have found to be profoundly helpful. First, forgive. Forgive yourself, in the case of your own transgressions, and forgive others if they have hurt you. How do you do this? Not by climbing up on your soapbox and in your righteousness saying, "I forgive myself, or you." You forgive yourself and anyone else who has hurt you simply by stopping the condemning judgments. Stop making condemning judgments about the observed discrepancies between your or the other person's behavior and the standard you have. For example, "I should always tell the truth." Yet you lied. Then you made your self-condemning judgment, and that unleashed the feelings of guilt. To let the guilt go, simply look on the event of your lying as something that happened. It simply happened; it is over; it is done; it is in the past. Simply observe the phenomenon in your mind, like a scientist or a journalist would. No judgment as to its badness, no editorializing, no moralizing over it; see it as something that was a historical event—period! If you do this, there is no condemning judgment; and if there is no condemning judgment, there is no guilt—that's how to forgive yourself.

Let's apply the process of letting go, of forgiveness, to a person's violation of a standard you are holding out for his or her behavior. Let's suppose you call on a prospect, and you have the rather irrational "should" in your head that every prospect you call on should buy your product. The present prospect ends the interview without manifesting any interest at all in your product. You leave, and you are angry—angry at the prospect, angry at the waste of time, angry at the other opportunities that you put on hold to talk to this person, and maybe even angry at yourself for not qualifying the prospect enough in advance. Now, if you were into pain and misery and wanted to be angry a lot, all you would have to do to bring on the angry feelings would be to run that videotape through your mind, and once again make that condemning judgment, i.e., "What a cheapskate, moron, bastard, louse, low-life he was." And what is the payoff? As if it happened yesterday, anger!

Now let's suppose you are not into prolonging your pain from the past into the foreseeable future. The process of letting go is the same as that you applied to the guilt example. Simply look on the event as having happened, and observe that it is over, done, history. Do not make a condemning judgment about the prospect, and what happens? The sluice gate opening the flood of feelings does not get raised, and a feeling disequilibrium does not occur. That's letting go. That's forgiveness. It does not deny what has happened; that can be acknowledged—but with no condemnation.

Peace and Serenity

What we experience internally is peace and serenity until we make ourselves miserable—guilty and angry. Peace is our natural state, but we need to replace the absurd meanings we use to guide our life, stop the condemning judgments, and get on with doing the things that lead to love, caring, and service. The payoff is that we will have tremendous energy to put into creativity and problem solving. Further, when I emphasize self and other forgiveness as the key, I am not advocating for a minute that you be morally obtuse, or that you not learn anything from your or another's deviance, or that you do not correct it, if possible, in order to restore equity—just the reverse. I am suggesting a way to get on with life without energy-sapping emotionalizations and move more readily into a problem-solving mode.

Summary and Bridge

The four great nemeses of salespeople have been identified, along with some strategies to counteract them. Fear is controllable, and need not inhibit anyone from doing the hard things or from taking a risk. Rejection needs to be reinterpreted as a positive experience and an indication that you are moving in the right direction. Again, what you believe about something will be your experience. But most importantly, you can control that and change hurtful or dumb beliefs into life-enhancing ones. Guilt and anger are gigantic balls and chains that really slow a person down and set him or her up for a distressful life. They will surely increase the chances of a life of anesthestics. Forgiving yourself and others is the key to getting on with life and not letting past behavior, however hurtful, immoral, or just plain stupid, dictate your feelings in the present moment. If you don't take the steps to jettison these things, you will be fated to mediocrity the rest of your life. It's more fun to be in the star category, and in the long run, easier. In fact, it takes more energy to make yourself miserable. Let's take the path of least resistance and live life from a posture of serenity, reasonable beliefs, and good feelings. Achievement will be the result. The reinforcing ripples will reverberate throughout your mind and your body, and give a lift to your experience of life that will be amazing to see.

The next chapter builds on these discussions and extends them to the relationships you have with others.

12

It's All About Relationships

	Yes	*No*
1. Would you like to understand why people behave the way they do?	☐	☐
2. Would you like others to seek you out?	☐	☐
3. Would you like to improve your relationships with your spouse, children, coworkers, and customers?	☐	☐

Let's start with an assertion. Every person has a crying fundamental need to feel special. We know that touch is as necessary for an infant's growth and development as food and drink. If a little baby is not touched, fondled, and caressed, that child will literally wither away, deteriorate, and, in extreme cases, actually die. This was researched back in 1945 by Rene Spitz, and the research results, the incredible consequences of touch or the lack of it, have been replicated many times since. However, as you grow older, your need for touch tends to get modified, since you can't go around touching all the people you would like to touch, or being touched by all the people you would like to be touched by. The basic survival need gets modified to a need for recognition. And it is also true for you and for me that if we do not get the recognition that we need, long for, and desire, our spinal cords will shrivel up, and in extreme cases we too will die.

Think about it. What is the worst punishment invented by jailers? It is not the whip, the lash, or the thumbscrew. The worst human punishment is solitary confinement. What is the biggest problem that old people have? It is not poor health, but loneliness, which eventually leads to poor health. For example, the death of widows and widowers in the 65–66 age bracket within one year of the death of their spouse is ten times greater than that of their married counterparts in the same age bracket. Why? Loneliness is the great killer.

Why is recognition so important? It not only stimulates a person's biochemical constitution but affirms the existence, the significance of that person. Some psychologists call this recognition event a stroke—giving a person a stroke. It has the connotations of touch, but it is fundamentally psychological; yet it has an effect comparable to that of physical stroking on an infant. The interesting thing is that there are different kinds of strokes a person can give or get that can affirm the other's existence—some are positive and life-enhancing, and generate warm feelings; and others are negative, hurtful, and destructive, and generate bad feelings.

To ascertain what kinds of strokes people are into, take a look at their self-worth. Do they see themselves as 10s or not? The 10s in the world regularly give themselves positive strokes, and that is what they regularly give to others. If you remember the argument about the business the 2s are into, namely, finding ways to be miserable, then you will see that the kinds of strokes those who see themselves as less than 10s give themselves and others regularly are negative.

What I am talking about here is communication—what you communicate to others, and what others communicate to you. Since I am of the school of thought that says, "Worry about the things you can control," the focus here will be on what you can do to communicate in a caring manner. Since you will reap what you sow, as the lonely old people have, if you communicate in a caring manner, that is what will come back to you from others. If you characteristically communicate in an uncaring manner, it is guaranteed that you will wind up lonely, and that folks will want to avoid you.

The major ways you have of delivering strokes are through what you say and what you do. Everything you say and do is communication in some manner, shape, or form. A way to know whether you are operating on an ethical humane plane is to simply use the Golden Rule as your fundamental guide and standard. It will dispose you to all the rewards you ever need, and show you how to behave in a caring manner. As you know, the Golden Rule is: "Do unto others as you would want others to do unto you." Below I have sketched out some guidelines for your consideration. If you do these things, you will reap the results of the questions you gave a yes to above.

Golden Rule Communication

When the Golden Rule is applied to communication, there are two key dimensions, each of which has its own imperatives, if you would like to be a model of it. The Golden Rule of communication is: "Speak to others as you would like to be spoken to, and listen to others as you would like to be listened to."

Let's take the second first, listening. It is first because it is what I call the "superstroke." Remember what I said earlier about how each of us has a crying need for recognition. One of the basic ways you can give that to other people is by giving them air time, by letting them tell their story, by letting them ventilate their emotions and viewpoints. If you are one of those uncommon persons on the planet who know how to do this, you will never be lonely yourself, because people will seek you out and welcome you when you visit. When you listen, you are in a position to help another feel understood, valued, and appreciated. It makes you a listening person, providing the superstroke, and it helps the other to feel like a 10. A listening person is a caring person. A caring person is a loving person. And although we don't tend to talk about love in business, when you listen to your customer, your coworker, your boss, your spouse, your child, you are indeed expressing love in the most intimate human way possible. When you listen with an eye to understanding, the other person starts sharing his or her innermost feelings and concerns with you. When you treat another person with sensitivity without judging, analyzing, or criticizing him or her, something incredible happens in the relationship—the other person begins to *trust* you. That's how you achieve trust and make it grow in a relationship: by listening with acceptance, by giving the other person air time without fear of being blown out of the water. And when trust occurs in a relationship, you can sell that person what he or she needs: you can guide, you can direct, or educate him or her. But when trust does not occur, selling is simply a question of price. In parenting, you are talking to a wall. In a marriage, this is the prelude to deceit. Friendships never get off the ground. How do you develop trust in a relationship? By listening to the other person. How do you do it?

• *Follow your biology, and your ear-to-mouth ratio 2:1.* (Two ears to one mouth. Listen twice as much as you speak.) If you look at how often people speak compared to how often they actually listen, you would swear that most folks had two mouths and one ear. Speaking is in. Listening is hard, and most people are not good at it at all. Think of the times when you were troubled in your own life. You longed to tell your story to somebody, and there was no one there. It is not by chance that people will spend $125 an hour to go to their local psychiatrist. It is because finding anyone to listen is a rare human experience, so rare that troubled people pay big bucks to a therapist when all that person fundamentally does is listen. So, if you do nothing else except follow your ear-to-mouth ratio, you will be a unique person.

You might wonder why people talk so much and listen so little. There are many reasons, but I have a hunch that most folks are so into themselves, their own trials and travails, ideas, goals, and plans, that you hardly register on their interest meter. They simply don't care; they are really not interested in your story, and they find the time when you are talking taxing. Most people are, in my judgment, so desperate to talk about themselves and to feel reassured that they are important that they literally go around looking for lapels to grab (so they can hold your attention). Knowing this fact and filling this need in a way that enhances your sales or your persuasive ability is not manipulation. It is simply good commercial sense; you find a need in the marketplace, and you fill it. Psychiatrists are not typically considered to be manipulators, nor are other therapists. All they are doing is filling a basic human need to feel valued. So if a salesperson knows that listening to a customer ingratiates him to a customer and makes the customer like him and therefore buy more from him, it is not crooked for the salesperson to be a listener. Nor is it manipulation for a salesperson to become a skilled listener; it is simply common sense on the part of the salesperson.

• *Ask open-ended questions.* It is one thing to know that it is wise to listen, and even to want to do so, but how do you get a person to talk? Ask questions, but not closed-ended questions that require only a monosyllabic answer, such as, What is your name? Where do you live? Are you in sales? How long have you been doing it? Are you married? Do you like it? Do you work in the city? A series of questions of this kind will make the recipient begin to feel you have him or her in an interrogation room under a white light. Now, I don't mean to say you should never ask a closed-ended question; sometimes you need a specific answer in order to explore the response with an open-ended question. For example, you ask, "Do you work in the city?" And the other person responds, "Yes." Then you follow it up with an open-ended question: "How do you feel about your safety working there?" You can see by the way the open-ended question is phrased that the respondent probably would not simply give a one-word answer, but would elaborate on the response. But even if the respondent said, "Good," you could follow it up with, "In what sense do you mean good?" You get the drift? Open-ended questions are invitations to the other person to develop a response. A few examples of this are: What happened next? Tell me about it. Describe it. How did you feel about that? And then . . . ? And after? How did you interpret that? What do you think that meant? How else could you have done it? What other options were available? What these questions do is tell the person that you want to hear the whole story, that they have air time, that you are eagerly waiting for the next aspect of their tale, that you want to *understand* what they are saying.

Not too many people can resist the invitation to talk about

themselves, their feelings, their experiences, their viewpoints. When you show interest like this, you will immediately be liked by the other person. In fact, the hallmark of a great conversationalist is that that person is a great listener. So if you ever wondered what to say in a social gathering or in a sales interview, don't ever worry again; all you have to do is to ask open-ended questions, and you will leave the other person with the best possible impression of you. Why? Because you are giving them the superstroke and the single most basic thing they need: "Someone is interested in me; someone cares about me and my life!"

• *Allow others to paint their picture.* Follow this metaphor. A person talking is like an artist painting a picture. Your job is to get the person to paint his or her picture in its entirety. He or she can paint it only when talking. When the person has finished, you can step back and see the picture. To the extent that you have allowed the other person to talk, the picture is complete. When the picture is fully developed through the other person talking, then that person will feel you understand. *Understanding is what people need!* You give them that simply by reflecting to them the pictures they have painted.

If you interrupt as someone is talking, say things like, "That reminds me of my first letter of rejection. It happened back in . . . ," and go on and on, you pull the paintbrush out of the person's hand. When it's all over, the picture is yours, not the other person's, and not much understanding has been rendered to the other person. Also, if as the person is talking you criticize, analyze, blame, or lecture, again understanding stops, and it will not be a satisfactory experience for that person.

• *To achieve rapport, mirror without mimicking.* When you mirror back to people the words and phrases (and paraphrases) they use, part of the picture they painted or the whole picture, they will feel you understand them. When you mirror back their feelings that you see, intuit, or sense, you are getting at the deepest level of understanding. "You feel sad about that?" "I'll bet you were angry when that happened."

But you can also mirror back their physiology—their posture, their movements, their gestures. Unconsciously they begin to see themselves in you, and feel better about you. What develops in this mirroring is rapport. Rapport is a comfort with you, a likableness about you, a feeling of a kindred spirit. Rapport comes as a consequence of being not intimidating but understanding, and from this the foundation of trust is built. It is important to do this naturally, not like a mime or in any way making fun of the speaker. Otherwise it is all over.

• *Give the other your focused attention.* Have you ever been in a dialogue with another person when that person is not giving you his or her focused attention? The person's eyes are roaming across the ceiling, or looking out into the parking lot. He or she is drumming the fingers of the right hand up and down, taking all incoming telephone calls, or reading a report while you are trying to explain your very delicate matter. Well, any one of those is an indicator that the other person is giving you only partial attention. If you really want to value another person, then choose an environment where there are no interruptions, where you can sit opposite the other person and periodically look her in the eyes and nod your head, showing that as she is telling you her story, you are with her.

• *Practice listening.* Listening is a skill. The way to develop any skill is by practice. Practice listening with your spouse. (If you practice it with your children, it will really test your mettle.) Practice it with your coworkers, and please, practice it with customers. You will discover a new magnetism about yourself. You will discover that your relationships with all these others in your life will improve. And practice it the rest of your life. A little exercise you can do is this: First, become acutely aware when a person is not listening to another person he or she is in a dialogue with. Watch a soap opera or a movie—it is the basis for conflict in these dramas, so look for these negative examples. Second, in your work and daily life, notice the frequency with which people turn others off, criticize, judge, discount others, and do *not* listen to their story. And third, seek out opportunities yourself to listen to others.

Speaking

Speaking is the other dimension to communication. If you speak to others the way you like to be spoken to, you will notice a transformation in your relationships with others. If you operate on the assumption that everyone is a 10 and that each of us has a fundamental need to feel valued and special, then it is useful to know how to fill that need better. Below are some suggestions on how to do so. You can use these with prospects, customers, family, and friends.

• *Start with your self-talk. As a general principle, celebrate yourself—your own personal worth and value—by making your self-talk life-enhancing.* Every day say yes to yourself and your opportunities. Let go of the self-condemning judgments, the invidious comparisons, and rehearsals of past or future miseries. Start your day with MRE, combine it with RAVE, and get on with a productive, feel-good, passionate day. Your core of good feeling and energy will color everything that comes out of your mouth, and send positive ripples that will uplift others.

• *Be a master at giving feedback.* Others in your life need to know where they stand all the time. So make your observations timely, as close to an event as possible. Don't put others in a position where they have to read your mind to know where they stand. Mind reading is misreading, and the probability of error is high when a person has to resort to it. So avoid confusion and uncertainty, and make your observations about them and their behavior timely and accurate. Be honest with them, be straight, but communicate. This principle is related to the next, more specific, recommendation.

• *Routinely catch people doing something right—and tell them!* We learn from B. F. Skinner that you can condition behavior by positive rewards or by punishment, but that you increase the likelihood of a behavior's not being repeated by ignoring it. So, if someone has done something good or appropriate and you ignore that behavior, you lessen the likelihood that it will be repeated. Expected or desired behavior needs to be reinforced positively, if you want it to continue. Suppose, for example, that on Monday night your beloved spouse cooks a gourmet meal for you, investing hours of time. You sit down to eat and do not make one comment about the meal. What is the likelihood that your spouse will cook a gourmet meal for you on Tuesday night? Slim to none. It is too easy and too common for folks to criticize behavior when something is wrong, and some people make a way of life out of that. But the key to great relations with your children, your spouse, your customers is to catch them doing something right and stroke them for it. It is not that we do it just to get them to do it again, but because in that act of giving the other a positive stroke, you are fulfilling a profound need each of us have—*to feel appreciated.* By flagging that event, you are acting in a caring, loving manner.

• *Praise in public; reprimand in private.* Each of us has a profound need to be recognized, so when occasions arise for recognizing another for outstanding performance, do it in public because the number of strokes given is multiplied by the number of people in the audience. Thus a positive stroke gets amplified in intensity, and all the more elates the person receiving the strokes. For the very same reason, reprimands in public are likewise multiplied in intensity, and in that act of mortification a person loses face and is humiliated. In my judgment, it is not a good idea to reprimand in public because it will engender profoundly hateful feelings on the part of the person being reprimanded, which may, in fact, come back to haunt you.

• *Eliminate sarcasm.* Eliminate the sarcastic lilt attached to your statements, judgments, and questions because it thinly veils a condemning "dummy" message. Sarcasm is an attack; it is a condemnation attached to the intonation of a person's voice that is simply designed to put the person at whom the question is directed in a one-down position. Use of sarcasm is not likely to lead to a sale, or affection, or good feelings in a relationship. In fact, it puts people off, and the receiver of the sarcasm will want to head for the door. So if you want lower sales, want less intimacy in a relationship, and thrive on loneliness, use sarcasm. If you don't, become sensitive to the disguised "dummy" messages you send and expunge them from your repertoire. The chapter on criticism will deal with this at greater length.

• *Be generous with your strokes.* Be generous with your strokes because you can't give them away. They always come back. For example, if I smile at you, what are you likely to do back at me? Smile. If I am kind to you, you are likely to be kind to me. Sometimes the return strokes come in entirely unexpected ways. For example, many years ago I gave a five-week seminar for a church as a fund-raiser. It met on Sunday nights. I received no compensation; I just did it because I knew that I had things to teach that would benefit the attendees, and that it would be a lot of fun. So I donated my time, with no strings attached. Over the next year, as a consequence of referrals that came from that course, I contracted for seminars at Bell Labs, Systems Control, Johnson & Johnson, and three school districts. I learned from this experience that you cannot give it away. What you give comes back a hundredfold, and often in ways and at times that you never expected. I would emphasize that generosity is a good policy, not just because you get back more than you give, but because it is a good thing to do in itself. There is something almost mystical in this concept of generosity. If you have been a mite stingy of late, give it up, and see the result.

• *Use the person's name.* The sweetest sound in any language is the sound of a person's own name. So when you are giving a stroke to someone, always use his or her name. A person's name is intimately associated with his or her historic identity, and on balance, most people have fond feelings attached to their own name. When you use a person's name, you have personalized whatever comes next for that person alone. The name gets the person's attention. It can break through all the other sounds in a conversation and reach out to the person in an emotional manner. The name and the person are one. Therefore, when you use a person's name in speech or in writing, always make sure it is correct. A mistake in a person's name is a profound discount. Just as you do not like anyone to mangle your name, no one else likes it when his or her name gets mangled. If you are not sure of the name or of the correct pronunciation or title, ask (preferably before the encounter).

As a hobby, develop your ability to remember the names of the people you meet. If you have found yourself saying, "I just can't remember names," please jettison that belief. The fact is, you simply have not invested the energy to do so or learned a technique that can be helpful. Here are a few pointers.

First, when you meet someone new, immediately associate his or her name with something wild, weird, or bizarre (Don't tell that person what the association is—it might get you in trouble.) You see, the brain works on the principle of association, and it remembers vivid pictures placed in the imagination more readily than abstractions like names. So what you do is to link the name, an abstraction, to something wild, weird, or bizarre and the person's features so that you will remember the name. Suppose you wanted to remember Leonid Brezhnev. Look at him, imagine a lion (Leo) brushing its hair, and associate the picture with Leonid Brezhnev's face. The next time you meet Leonid, the picture of the lion brushing its hair will pop immediately into your mind. His name will follow right after. Or, one more example, suppose the name of the customer is Weldon Rackley. Picture a welder welding a rack of lamb. When you meet Weldon, the picture will effortlessly come to the fore, and your brain will link the more abstract name to it. Test it out. And second, use the name as often as you can immediately after the introduction. It will help to reinforce it in your memory.

• *Be specific.* When you deliver a stroke, make it specific and concrete, as opposed to general and sweeping. This is true whether it is a positive comment or a criticism. A statement like, "You do good work" is nice, but a statement like, "John, the report you gave me yesterday saved my life at the meeting; I really appreciated it" is specific, concrete, and vastly more believable. So, please make your "Attaboy(s)" more believable.

• *Criticism.* Although I have consistently come down on criticism as the most destructive thing that can go on between two people, there are times when criticism is warranted and necessary. In those cases, it is important to communicate the criticism in a believable, rational manner. How do you do it? Start your criticism off with the person's name, followed by the word *when;* for example, "John, when you are late for the meeting, it forces me to lose valuable time." Because of the way the English language is structured, using *when* as I did above forces you to describe the behavior that is bothering you and the effects of that behavior. The beauty of this type of critical format is that the statement is targeted at the behavior and not at the person.

You will find a hundred opportunities to test this format out. Start at home with your spouse, children, or family members, and you will see that it engenders an entirely different response from an overt attack, a "dummy" message, or sarcasm.

• *Evaluating someone else.* When you are evaluating another's behavior, use Mamie Taylor's three questions. Mamie Taylor was a master teacher in Dallas, and periodically she would have to evaluate a young student teacher's lesson. At the end of the student's practice lesson, Mamie would have the young student sit down for the evaluation. Much to the student's surprise, Mamie would ask the following three questions:

> *What did you do right?* The student would naturally expect Mamie to run through a checklist of all the things done wrong. This question was totally disarming and unexpected. It also put the student at ease and set the tone for a friendly event.
>
> *If you had it to do over again, what would you do differently?* Well, since we are typically our own worst critics, the student would typically give a self-critique that covered not only the defects in the lesson, but ideas on how to correct them. It is generally a superior learning experience for a person to identify the problem and possible solutions, rather than having an authority figure provide them.
>
> *What can I do to be helpful?* Here Mamie was making herself available for help, information, and support. This was truly a caring invitation.

Test these three questions out. You can use them any time you are in a counselling or coaching session with anyone—a customer, a coworker, a family member. I have, for example, often used them with my two sons as they were growing up, and it has helped significantly to show that I value them, care for them, and want to see them be even better. Best of all, it generates none of the bad feelings associated with correction and criticism.

• *Help others feel special.* If you want the key to demonstrating to others that they truly are important, periodically sit down and raise this question: "How can I help _____ feel special today?" If this person is your customer, spouse, child, friend, coworker, or relative, and you do brainstorm some strategies and then, in fact, act on them, you have a method that will improve any relationship you have.

Summary and Bridge

The Golden Rule is applied to communication, and guidelines for listening and speaking are spelled out. In general, people need to be positively stroked as much as they need food to eat and water to drink. Therefore, when an opportunity arises, do the magnanimous thing and give a positive stroke. When it is necessary to criticize, package it in a caring manner. What you are doing is defining your relationships as an opportunity to give, to help, to provide, to serve. When you do, the rewards will be so self-evident that you will wonder why you did not adopt this strategy of relating earlier.

The next chapter deals with the darker side of relationships and presents strategies for dealing more effectively with manipulators.

13

Criticism and the Teflon Salesperson

	Yes	No
1. Do you know any manipulators?	☐	☐
2. Is it important for you to deal more effectively with them?	☐	☐
3. Would you like to learn how to be unflappable in the face of criticism?	☐	☐

Just as a yes is what a salesperson lives for, and connotes everything that is positive, good, and rewarding, a no is painful, and it takes real skill at interpretation not to get blown out of the water when it occurs. Hopefully the guidance above on dealing with a no helps. However, there is another dimension to a no, beyond the sales transaction or cold calling effort, that needs to be explored. All criticism we receive is essentially a no, a rejection, a condemnation. Noes and criticism are among the hardest things for a person to deal with. Think of the times when you have been criticized. Think of the things you have been criticized about—your work, your appearance, your viewpoints, your weight, your beliefs, your

feelings, your education or lack of it, your lifestyle, your occupation, your politics, your religion, your ethics, etc. Think about who
did it, what they said, and how you felt. About 80 percent of the
time, when you are criticized, it is not done in a kindly way, with
an eye to helping you to grow and develop as a person. It is designed to denigrate, put down, hurt, demolish, control, and dictate
what you should or should not do. No matter how you look at it,
the critic is saying no to something about you.

Most of the time you are caught off guard when you are criticized. However, if you inspect the behavior of others who criticize
you, you will soon discover that there is a pattern to it. Many folks
are into a critical, judgmental mindset, and once you discover who
they are and when they do their nastiness, you will be able to predict their behavior in the future. Scientists and engineers know that
things that you can predict, you can control. In this instance, you
will not be able to prevent another from attacking, but you can
always control your response to it. That's what you will learn here:
how to control your response to criticism of you, regardless of
whether this is the first or the tenth time it has occurred. The principles and strategies below can help you when you are confronted
with *difficult* prospects and customers. They can also arm you in
the struggle with all those other "crooked" folks who use criticism
as their weapon of choice to control you.

First of all, it is useful to know what is happening when someone delivers a criticism to you. In most cases of criticism, what you
have is manipulation, but you may not be aware that you are being
manipulated. What the manipulative critics are saying is this: According to *their* standard of right and wrong, what you are doing
is wrong. They are saying that your behavior is not in conformity
with *their* standard; you are bad or wrong, and ought to feel guilty
about it, until you bring your behavior into conformity with *their*
standard. What manipulators are doing is denying you your freedom to determine what *your* standards of right and wrong will be.
In effect, manipulators are saying that you are supposed to guide
your life according to *their* standards.

Why do they do this? I think it has everything to do with how
they feel about themselves, which is to say that you can bet that
they surely do not feel like 10s or know that they are 10s, and they
are not comfortable around folks who do know that they are 10s.

So one reason why they attack is to make you, for one fleeting moment of time, more miserable than they are. If they can make you feel bad, then, by comparison, they are not so badly off. This invidious relief from pain is brief, so they have to continue their attack or find someone else to make miserable. At the end of their day you can find a wake of dead bodies. They may have learned this strategy from their own parents and simply not know any better. But one sure consequence of it is that it prevents anyone from getting close to them. It is like they are straight-arming everyone they deal with. The payoff for them is little affection, love, or intimacy, and lots of bad feelings.

Another reason why people manipulate others is because they feel that those others either are too dumb to do the right thing or can't be trusted to do the right thing without their guidance. Their motivation could also be rooted in the fear that you might be hurt or ridiculed, or slip into a big problem, which, of course, you could avoid if you did it their way. Thus manipulation can come from the most nurturant motivation or the most crass self-centeredness. In some sense, the motivation doesn't matter, because it has the same effect on the person on the receiving end of the criticism. It hurts; it's a no; it's a condemnation.

What About Your Rights?

I want you to get in touch with your rights. First, who is responsible for your life? I hear you say, "I am." Who is responsible for your happiness? I hear you say, "I am." Who is responsible for your behavior? Once again, "I am." And finally, who is responsible for determining what your personal standards of right and wrong will be? I heard you say, "I am."

Great; now, with this understanding of your rights in mind, you need to understand what the component parts of a criticism are, and then from that analysis a strategy for dealing with criticism in an unflappable manner will be developed. However, the methodology I will teach you will be what I believe is a morally superior way of responding. First, all of you know how to fight. You know how to attack people back, and even in a more devastating way than they attacked you. All of you know how to cuss, use sarcasm, and send a verbal stiletto that can silence the critic. I am not saying never to use that method of defending yourself; you may find that some circumstances do warrant that type of response. But strangely, that is exactly the response that some critics want to elicit from you, and when you give it, they have in fact controlled your feelings, pressed your hot button, and gotten you upset. You are going to learn a method in the tradition of Martin Luther King, Mahatma Gandhi, and those other self-contained individuals who know the game the provocateurs are into. It is a game they don't deign to play. Your response will be so powerful, you never even have to defend yourself.

The Critic's Weapons

A critic has two weapons: not-real questions and overt criticism. Let's look at not-real questions. They look like questions, but they reek with sarcasm, and have unspoken at the end, in parentheses, the word *dummy*. In fact, a not-real question is a no about your behavior; it is a condemning judgment. For example, "Do you have to comb your hair that way?" "Do you always come to meetings ten minutes late?" "Do you really need to be so aggressive?" Let me repeat those questions, but this time explicitly add the *dummy* refrain that goes with the intonation, the sarcastic lilt: "Do you have to comb your hair that way, (dummy)?" "Do you always come to meetings ten minutes late, (dummy)?" "Do you really need to be so aggressive, (dummy)?" These questions are subtle, because if you call a critic delivering one of these sarcasms on it, you will get the response, "I was only asking a question." But this is not really the case, because the real message is in the intonation, and that message is a "dummy" message, a negating, condemning one. If you put the not-real question into a simple declarative sentence in which the deliverer took ownership of the statement, the three examples above would look like: "I don't like the way you comb your hair." "I hate it when you are late for a meeting." "I don't care for your aggressiveness at all." But the interesting thing about manipulators using not-real questions is that they *don't* take ownership of their viewpoints, and they relinquish that responsibility by asking a question. The way a question functions is that it puts all the pressure on the person at whom the question is directed. It puts an obligation on that person to respond, or to defend his or her behavior. In the act of asking a question, a manipulator thus transfers the responsibility for explaining to the other person while simultaneously condemning that person's behavior.

How do you deal with not-real questions when they are put to you? It is simple: Answer them literally and briefly. So to the question, "Do you have to comb your hair that way?" a literal and brief response would be, "No." That's it! No explanation, no defense, no affect, no interrogation of the asker's motives—just, "No," and nothing else. Likewise, to, "Do you always come to meetings ten minutes late?" simply respond, "No"—period; no explanation. And to, "Do you really need to be so aggressive?" you could simply say, "Yes." That's it—nothing else. I can assure you that this monosyllabic reply will put the manipulator off and be a total surprise. You are responding to the question on the literal level when the real message is in the intonation, but manipulators cannot accuse you of not responding to their real message, because then they would unmask themselves. What you do, in effect, is send them a message that tells them that you see through their crookedness.

So, here is your homework. Listen to the not-real questions people use on one another. Make an effort to be straightforward, and when you ask questions, let them be real ones, searching for real information. And finally, when someone puts a not-real question at your door, answer it literally and briefly—"Yes," "No," "Maybe," "Sometimes" (whatever the appropriate brief response would be), and that's it.

Overt Criticism

Manipulators are not dumb. When they criticize you, there is usually some truth that you could tease out of their statement, but they take that truth fragment and attach it to their standard of right and wrong. For example, look at these critical statements: "You look like Bozo the Clown in that outfit." "You can't do anything right." "Your presentation was a disaster." "You're going to get into trouble if you stay out that late." Your strategy for dealing with these criticisms is to separate the truth or the probability from the statement and reject their standard of right and wrong while preserving your right to act in a way that is consistent with your own standard. It sounds complicated, but let me show you. When someone criticizes you, you can respond using the simple format below:

It's true, + you qualify in what sense the statement is true.

It might be, + you qualify in what sense the observation might be.

It could be, + you qualify in what sense the truth fragment could be.

It's possible, + you qualify in what sense the observation is possible.

So let's take, "You look like Bozo the Clown in that outfit." You might dig out this truth from the sweeping criticism: "It's true, it is a very playful outfit." There is no way you believe you look like Bozo the Clown, but you do know that clowns are associated with fun, and you can accept as true that aspect of the statement. Remember, manipulators expect you to get upset, defensive, and embarrassed, and to go upstairs and change your outfit into something more pleasing to their esthetic taste. When you tease playfulness out of their criticism and accept that, it nonplusses them; they don't expect it, and at the same time you are asserting your decision to wear anything you choose. Or to, "You can't do anything right," you might say: "It's true, on occasion I do make mistakes." You know, in fact, that you do not *always* make mistakes. That you cannot accept, but you can accept the truth that on occasion you do make mistakes. Again, the response is not what the critic is looking for. Or to, "Your presentation was a disaster," you might say: "You know, there were quite a number of things I would do differently in retrospect." Let's suppose that your presentation was not as good as it could have been, but you know that it was not, in fact, a disaster. Your response accepted its improvability, not that it was a disaster. Or to, "You're going to get into trouble staying out that late," you might say, "It is possible that I could get into trouble being out that late." You know it is in no way certain that you will get in trouble staying out late, but you also know that in the scheme of life, it is possible that staying out

late could lead you into trouble. What you do is reserve for yourself whether you are going out at that hour or not.

In each one of these instances, you are trying to tease out a
truth fragment that you can accept, and then qualify in what precise sense you do accept it. In every instance you maintain your
right to act or not act, believe or not believe, change or not change.
You assert your right to guide your behavior, beliefs, values, feelings, and actions according to your own standards of right and
wrong. You do not accept the critic's standard of right and wrong.
In fact, you ignore it.

Practice

Once you understand the analysis above, start practicing it in low-
risk situations, in your family, for instance, and then move into
other arenas where you may come across manipulators and where
more is at stake.

When Your Brain Is Like Jelly

Let's suppose you are criticized by someone and you don't want
to get into combat, but you can't think of any of the preceding
responses. You could always do variations on this theme: *I can understand* that viewpoint.

> *I can understand* why you might feel that way.
> *I can understand* your concern.
> *I can understand* how you could interpret it that way.

In this statement, you are not saying that you agree or disagree or
that you are going to do what the critic wants you to do. You are
simply stating that you understand what the critic is saying, but
you will, again, reserve your right to do whatever you choose.

A More Aggressive Approach

When someone makes a criticism of you and you want to take a
more vigorous position that will eventually extinguish the manipu-

lation and put the critic on notice that you are one person who will not be manipulated, use this format:

> *I don't understand*—in what sense is my outfit like Bozo the Clown?
> *I don't understand*—in what sense do I always make mistakes?
> *I don't understand*—in what sense was my presentation a disaster?
> *I don't understand*—in what sense is being out that late going to cause trouble?

In each one of the instances above, the person will typically come up with another implausible, nonfactual, sweeping overgeneralization that will not stand up under scrutiny. And when that happens, simply say once again, sincerely, "I don't understand." And again and again. Finally the person will see the fatuity of his or her own position, and say to you, "Forget it; you wouldn't understand even if I could explain it to you." Or the person might just leave. But in any event, the critic knows for sure that you are one person whose buttons he or she cannot press.

Your style in doing this more aggressive inquiry is to be gentle and slow, with genuine puzzlement and a sincere searching. I don't want you to be obnoxious, but following this regimen can help you to put the obnoxious manipulator on the defensive. Again, start your skill development in low-risk situations. I don't want you to get fired, or get a black eye.

What if What They Say Is True?

Some criticism that others give you is valid, and could be helpful. I would hope that you are smart enough to take good advice wherever you can get it. You and I do not have a monopoly on wisdom, and on occasion we actually do dumb things, make mistakes, screw up, or operate on half truths, to our own detriment. So when others do offer their input to you, consider it. Don't immediately discount it; weigh it, and if it can help you improve, use it. It's a wise man or woman who does that. Finally, take the chip off your shoulder, deep-six the arrogance, and display the humility of a seeker.

Summary and Bridge

You understand why folks criticize, the effects of criticism, and how to distinguish constructive criticism from manipulative criticism. You learned that the world is populated by manipulators in every area of life, work, family, and friendship relationships, and that manipulators sometimes are acting out of real love and caring, but sometimes simply out of the need to control you. Regardless of their motivation, you now have a set of tools for dealing with not-real questions and overt criticism. Applying these, you will not only be a Teflon salesperson, but you will see that most criticisms from others will slide right off you. You also know how to extinguish manipulation, and, of course, accept constructive criticism. Further, if you hold the mirror up to yourself, you may have an "aha" experience and discover that on occasion you may have been a manipulator. Now you know how *not* to go down that path.

The next chapter explores further kinds of conflict that people get implicated in, and spells out some strategies for coping better.

14

Conflict and Negotiation

	Yes	*No*
1. Do you experience much conflict in your life?	☐	☐
2. Is it important to you to learn how to deal better with it?	☐	☐
3. Would you like to become a better negotiator?	☐	☐

What Is a Conflict?

The Latin roots of the word suggest its essence. *Con* is from *cum*, which means "with," and *flictus* is a noun that means "striking together." So by definition, a conflict is a struggle with another. A struggle is invariably over something—something one party has that the other wants and that is not readily forthcoming. In a conflict, we have, therefore, a discrepancy between a need and its fulfillment. In fact, when the need gets fulfilled or abandoned by one party, the conflict ends for that party.

Conflicts among humans are rarely dispassionate. They almost always generate emotion (from mild to intense), and they are ubiquitous. Wherever people interact, conflicts occur. Why? Because of the sheer frequency with which one person wants something from another that is not forthcoming. The reverse of conflict is harmony, balance, fulfillment, smooth interpersonal relationships, and peace. How often do we either observe this state or experience it ourselves? It seems it is the exception rather than the rule.

So, since it appears that conflict is part of the human condition, and it is unrealistic to even try to banish it from our lives, the rational questions are, how can you lessen the frequency of it, and when it occurs, how can you increase your chances of resolving it effectively? That's what this chapter is all about.

For a Salesperson

To take this discussion out of the abstract, let's consider for a minute all the people with whom a salesperson might have a conflict. Write out the names of these folks here: _____

_____

Each one of these persons reflects a role he or she plays. The role of others with whom salespeople regularly come into conflict are prospects, customers, bosses, colleagues, sales support staff, factory personnel, spouses, children, sons, daughters, parents, in-laws, relatives, friends, vendors, service suppliers, professionals, government officials, neighbors, etc. Conflicts can occur with any one of these parties. The important question, however, is, when the conflicts do occur, what should you do about them? And an even more basic question is whether you should do anything.

Is It Worth It?

It takes a significant investment of time and energy to attempt to resolve a conflict. Sometimes you may, in fact, be trying to water a dry stick, hoping it will flower, when, in truth, it never will. That would be a fruitless waste of energy. It is necessary to ask yourself, "Is it worth it?" Ask this simply because not all battles are worth fighting. But if the answer to this is always no and you feel victimized and resentful because you are always on the losing end of a deal, then that is a clue that you are caving in prematurely and not standing up for your rights.

If your answer to the question is *almost* always no and you do not feel bad about the situation, then you may be a saint, or you may have either learned to live life more loosely than most folks or carefully chosen your fields of combat. Sainthood is rare, but one of the other two paths might, indeed, be more prudent. It is my judgment that not every disagreement you may have is worth taking umbrage over. Not every slight assault is worth throwing the gauntlet down or going to the mat over.

How do you decide which ones are and are not worth fighting for? Do a simple reward/cost analysis and compare the probability of the payoffs with the amount of time, energy, emotion, and inconvenience likely to be involved. You may still decide to charge ahead after this analysis, but it interrupts the Pavlovian response to combat that might occur if you did not pause to ask, "Is it worth it?" or the automatic retreat from a struggle if that is your usual way of reacting.

The Kinds of Conflict

Given a conflict, it is important to get a handle on precisely what kind of conflict is occurring. This will help in determining whether to move into action and, if so, what particular strategy to take.

There are two generic types of conflicts: those where what is at stake is concrete and tangible, and those where what is at stake is *not* concrete and tangible. When the issue at stake is not something that is concrete and tangible, it is typically a standards conflict. It is a conflict in an arena—standards, ideas, principles, taste, or preference, where a person makes a moral judgment—it's good; it's bad. On the other hand, many conflicts, particularly those in the sales area, have at stake concrete and tangible things, like money, time, quantity, price, energy, convenience, services, or products.

Conflicts in Standards

These conflicts occur in every area. Some examples of standards conflicts that occur where one person says, "It's good for me," and the other person says it is not, are:

Choice of sports team	Clothes you wear
Color preferences	Location of your home
Style preferences	Decor
Taste preferences	Many moral stances
Choice of schools to attend	Lifestyle preferences
Makeup	Beauty
Political party preferences	Many priorities
Religious preferences	Goals and dreams
Kind of car you drive	Philosophies of life

These conflicts flow out of issues of control and occur when one person tries to impose his or her standard (choice, value, belief, morality) on another, who has a different standard. What distinguishes a standards conflict is that there is nothing concrete, specific, or tangible at stake; the disagreement is in the area of ideas. There are two kinds of standards conflict: (1) those in which you are trying to get someone else to adopt your viewpoint, and (2) those in which someone is trying to get you to change your posture.

Course of Action

If you are trying to get your standard adopted, and what is at stake does not affect you in a concrete and tangible manner, *act as a consultant*. What does this mean? If a company asks me, as a consultant, to analyze its business, I research the organization, identify problems, and make recommendations. When I have done this, I convene a meeting with the decision makers and make as strong and persuasive a case as I can for those recommendations—once. I leave it up to them to adopt or not adopt my recommendations; it's their choice, but I only make my case *once*.

So when I say, in standards conflicts, act as a consultant, I mean that you should make your case for the rightness of your viewpoint as strongly and persuasively as possible, but make that case only *once*, and give the other person the freedom to choose. When you make your case again and again and again, that is what nagging is all about, and nagging is a sure-fire way to kill a relationship. So when your twenty-one-year-old son comes home from college with his lover, Joel, with whom he is living, and you are an orthodox conservative Baptist, what do you do? Act as a consultant to your son. Make your case, but tell him it will only be made once, and then let it go. I know your head is whirling on your shoulders over this, but think about it. The alternative is to make your case again and again, and that is guaranteed to distance you from your son—to such an extent that he may not want to talk to you again.

On the other hand, when someone is trying to impose a standard on you, what do you do? First, recognize that you have the right to determine your standards, tastes, and preferences in all things that do not harm others in any concrete and tangible way. Second, the strategy others use to manipulate you out of your freedom is criticism and overt and not-real questions. Simply adopt the strategies spelled out in the previous chapter and you will be unflappable.

When What Is at Stake Is Concrete and Tangible

The stake in this kind of conflict is not simply in the world of ideas. What is at stake is something you can see, feel, touch, or hear; something you can count and measure; something observable, such as money, time, energy, size, location, injury, or payoff. Whereas in a standards conflict, when an adversary says, "What difference does it make?" all a person can say is, "I don't like it," in a conflict with something concrete and tangible at stake, you can reply to the question, "What difference does it make?" with some precision, in dollars, units, or measures that are understandable.

Course of Action

In the kind of conflict where what is at stake is concrete and tangible, there are four main outcomes: win-lose, lose-win, lose-lose, and win-win. If the resolution of any conflict leaves either party in a losing position, it is guaranteed to come back to haunt you. What I advocate is to try and engineer a win-win resolution to a conflict. The method of doing this is negotiation. Below I have spelled out some guidelines that can help you engineer a win-win agreement. First of all, I have listed a series of questions that it would make sense for you to ask *prior* to any negotiation. This will help you to prepare sensibly for the actual eyeball-to-eyeball event.

Questions to Prepare for a Negotiation

1. What additional information do I need to know, and how can I get it?
2. If I am not dealing with a decision maker, how can I get to do so?
3. What interests do I have at stake in this negotiation?
4. What are the interests of the other party?
5. What are the areas of probable agreement?
6. What are a number of options that respond to the mutual interests at stake?
7. What objective criteria can be invoked as a standard of fairness?
8. What is my least acceptable position?
9. What is the likely result for me if no agreement is reached?
10. What is the likely result for the other party if no agreement is reached?

The Actual Negotiation Process

Remember, the result of a successful negotiation is the achievement of a mutually satisfactory agreeement consistent with the interests of each party. Arriving at an agreement is a process. It is a process of give and take; of asking, explaining, proposing, reframing, modifying, and eventually agreeing. A helpful way to do this is to keep these guidelines in mind:

1. *Throughout the process, separate the people and their style from the issue.* Maintain your focus, and don't be sidetracked by extraneous factors, particularly personalities.

2. *In the dialogue that ensues, always give your attention to satisfying the interests of the other party.* Interests refer to the big picture—a product that works, freedom from fear, confidence in solving the problem, security, mutual profitability, etc.

3. *To get on a roll, agree to points that are acceptable to each party first.* When a dispute occurs, table the issue and come back to it later, while continuing to nail down points of agreement. This applies the principle of positive momentum.

4. *Don't get hung up on detail or on a specific position; always go back to the interests.* That's where the possibility for a creative agreement lies. Actual cost or price, for example, can be the great deal killer; always go back to the big picture of interests.

5. *When dealing with a party's firm/intractable position, ask "why," "why, "why."* The reply will give you more information on the interests that other party has at stake. The other party is programmed to answer questions, and "why" is the magic one.

6. *When attacked, use benign techniques to extinguish manipulative criticism, refer to the big picture (interests), ask why, and give your attention to standards of fairness.* Standards of fairness refer to the going rate in your industry or a comparable program that allows you to maintain reasonableness in your position.

7. *Do not attack back, criticize, ridicule, or denigrate the position, manner, or motivation of the other party.* If you do, it lessens the likelihood of a win-win agreement and is simply unprofessional.

8. *When emotions get charged in a dialogue, it is usually desirable to take a break.* It is amazing what a simple change of focus does for all parties.

9. *Remember that there is never just one acceptable position for an agreement.* There is always another one—the one you haven't thought of yet.

10. *Generating many alternative proposals is the key to creative and more mutually satisfying agreements.* It provides a choice, and there is something positive and hopeful about having a variety of possibilities to chose from.

11. *It is usually desirable, but not always possible, to invite the other party into the solution of the problem based on the satisfaction of mutual needs.* The other party's input on the solution means that less time is spent on selling your solution than when you alone provide it.

12. *Your degree of flexibility in the negotiation will be conditioned by where you go if no agreement is reached at all.* It is always possible for a negotiation to break down. You have to consider where that will leave you and where it will leave the other party; that will dictate how tough or compromising you can be in the negotiation process.

13. *Do not put the relationship in jeopardy by engineering a win-lose agreement.* Resentment will occur, and it will be a one-sale relationship.

14. *After the agreement is cast, be generous.* Throw in an extra widget, or whatever, and the other party will feel good about you and the deal *after* the deal.

Negotiation Checklist

To make sure you have done what you can do, below is a simple checklist to remind you:

Negotiation Checklist

	Yes	No
1. Is it really negotiable?	☐	☐
2. Is it worth it to me?	☐	☐
3. Do I have enough information to do it well?	☐	☐
4. Am I dealing with a decision maker?	☐	☐
5. Am I separating the people involved in this from the issue(s) at stake?	☐	☐
6. Have I spelled out my interests in this?	☐	☐
7. Have I spelled out the interests of the other party?	☐	☐
8. Have I identified the agreeable points?	☐	☐
9. Have I come up with an array of options?	☐	☐
10. Do I know my least acceptable position?	☐	☐
11. Have I identified objective criteria for fairness?	☐	☐
12. Do I know my best alternative if no agreement is reached?	☐	☐
13. Do I know the other party's best alternative if no agreement is reached?	☐	☐
14. Have I thought about the environment for the meeting?	☐	☐
15. Have I written my answers to the negotiation preparation questions?	☐	☐

16. **Have I reviewed the negotiation communication notes?** ☐ ☐

Summary and Bridge

Conflict is everywhere. It is part of the human condition. There are two major kinds of conflict: those that are standards conflicts, where there are ideational differences in philosophy, taste, morals, views, etc., and those where what is at stake is concrete and tangible. In the former, it is desirable to act as a consultant, and in the latter, as a negotiator. The ideas proposed here lead to conflict resolution and have application in every relational arena, e.g., sales, coworkers, your family, friends, etc.

The next chapter extends this discussion of conflict to games. Games are nonaware strategies that tend to be nonproductive and distancing, and usually result in bad feelings. How not to go down that path will be spelled out.

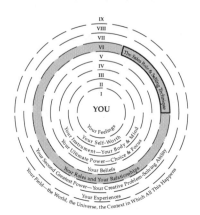

15

Games Salespeople Play

	Yes	No
1. Would you like to know why some encounters with others always result in acid indigestion?	☐	☐
2. Would you like to know whether you are into game playing?	☐	☐
3. Would you like to know how *not* to go down these crooked paths?	☐	☐

The games I am talking about here are not like checkers, chess, or backgammon. These games hurt, lead to bad feelings in a relationship, and impede one's personal effectiveness at work. They are a special kind of negative ripple. In order to understand the dynamics of a game and the payoffs associated with it, I will give you an example of one and analyze it. Once you understand that game, you will understand any game people play. Then I will apply the analysis to some of the games salespeople are known to play. Of course, the bottom line for you is to learn what you can do *not* to go down that path.

A Dialogue

Every so often the sales manager (SM) of the region would call Mr. Low Performing Salesman (LPS) into his office. The dialogue would go something like this:

SM: LPS, you said you wanted to see me?

LPS: Yes. I'm concerned about hitting my sales target; I'm having some problems.

SM: Well, why don't you spend more time out in the field? I'm sure that would help your numbers.

LPS: I would, but customers get angry if I'm not available when they call.

SM: Why don't you use the Daytimer to organize your time better?

LPS: That's a good idea, but I'm so busy keeping my customers satisfied, I don't have time to fool around with my Daytimer.

SM: Why didn't you consult with me earlier on your problem? I'm only here to help you succeed.

LPS: I would have, SM, but I'm already booking sixteen hours of work in an eight-hour day, and I do know how to sell, you know.

SM: I'm sure you do, but why don't you let me accompany you on a sales call? Maybe I could give you the benefit of my experience.

LPS: That's a good suggestion, but you know our sales approach is to build relationships with the customer, and having a third party butt in doesn't help to do that.

SM: Why don't you take this seminar I heard about on cold calling? It would surely help you get new business.

LPS: You know, maybe I will—next year. I just can't take time out now and run the risk of alienating my present customers.

SM: Well, at least take these tapes along and listen to them in your car.

LPS: Ordinarily I would hop at the chance, but I'm just getting into my cellular phone, and I'm trying to make my automobile an office on wheels.

SM: Well, LPS, everything I've suggested you have rejected. I'm fed up with you, your arrogance, and your block-headedness. Don't bug me anymore—and you better hit your numbers or your butt will be in a sling!

LPS: (Leaves the room, and goes out thinking what a jerk his boss is, how hard his selling job is, and how nothing ever goes right for him. He spends the rest of the day mollifying his bad feelings.)

SM: (Sits at his desk fuming, frustrated, and filled with feelings of antipathy toward LPS, and has a distinct sense that he has just been had, once again.)

Okay, the name of this game is YDU,YB, or "Why Don't You, Yes But." How do you know it is a game? There are three clues: (1) there are two parties involved, (2) the interaction ends with both parties experiencing bad feelings, and (3) both have been down this path before. Those are the three clues that you might be involved in a game. Now, how can you analyze a game?

First, in every game there are three poles, the Victim, the Perse-cutor, and the Rescuer. Each party in a game can play the game from one of the poles or move from one pole to another, while the other assumes a reciprocal posture; for example, one party acts like a Victim, hooking the Rescuer in the other party, or one party is the Persecutor while the other is the Victim, or the Rescuer might move to the Victim pole while the original Victim becomes the Persecutor.

Figure 3 is a simple graphic that highlights these three poles.

Let's go back to the dialogue and analyze it from a game per-spective. Notice how the game above starts. LPS defines himself as a Victim: "I have a problem." This statement hooks the Rescuer in SM, and he immediately starts sending solutions. But each solu-tion, "Why don't you," is rejected by LPS. What happens to SM? He starts feeling like a Victim, and perceives LPS as a Persecutor. Eventually SM has had enough of the frustration, and he slides over to the Persecutor pole and starts leveling his guns at LPS. LPS, as a consequence, now begins to feel like a double Victim; not only does he have a problem hitting his sales target, but now his boss is

Figure 3. The game triangle.

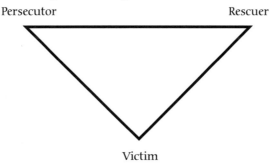

unjustifiably hollering at him. The game ends with both parties stuck at the Victim pole, suffused with feelings of frustration and bitterness. Each feels worse after this transaction than before it began. Nothing productive happened. Greater distaste for each other has resulted.

Other Games

A classic game many an LPS plays is Wooden Leg. This refers to a guy who goes to a party, and says, "You know, I would dance except I have a wooden leg." The wooden leg is the excuse for not dancing. Salespeople have all sorts of wooden legs that give them a reason not to perform adequately. Here's a sampling you may have heard around the office:

> "I'd be in the President's Club, but all my clients are in a down cycle."
> "I'd make my targets, but shipping keeps losing my orders."
> "I'd hit my goal, if only we had more up-to-date products."
> "I'd be among the stars, if I could give better discounts."
> "I'd be able to double sales, if I could get shorter lead times."
> "If only I had some decent leads, I could do vastly better."
> "If only I had a sales assistant, then I could spend prime time selling."

Statements of this kind are the plaintive cry of a Victim, one who is getting mileage out of being depressed and miserable, and in the process frustrating management. You know the person is a game player because if you were to outfit the wooden legger with a space-age prosthesis that would enable him or her to dance, the excuse would then be: "They never play my kind of music." Likewise, if you remove a particular wooden leg from a salesperson who is in the Victim slot, he or she will find another one. What you get are excuses, excuses, excuses, and, of course, it's never the salesperson's fault.

Self-Fulfilling Defeat

This is a game, once again, played by an LPS. The LPS is stuck in the Victim mode, and complains about how he or she never gets the sale. Looking at the LPS's performance when interacting with a prospect, what an objective observer sees is an attitude that drives prospects away. Sometimes it is sarcasm; sometimes a haughty, arrogant air; sometimes an "I'm doing you a favor by even dealing with you" demeanor; sometimes a nonverbal eye roll that makes the prospect feel dumb. The prospect experiences it as a put-down, and the salesperson is, in reality, in the Persecution mode. When the prospect walks out or ends the interview, the salesperson slides back into the Victim mode. Game players like this have, in fact, caused that which they are complaining about by their own behavior, although they deny responsibility for having done so.

Info-Mess

This is a game played by salespeople who often don't have enough time and are overwhelmed with paperwork. What they do, with some frequency, is to make errors when they are taking down the specifications from a customer, which they then convey to others in the order entry process, and ultimately to the factory. Invariably the errors are discovered, and the salespeople wind up redoing the order, correcting the errors, explaining to customers why they missed dates, and thus, having problems. Time is lost, and energy is consumed in a lot of nonproductive rectification. The salespeople naturally feel like Victims and become Persecutors to others in the order entry process, and much bad feeling results before matters get resolved, and that's only for the time being! You can often hear these same salespeople saying, "I'm just not a detail person—it's not my thing."

This kind of scenario can lead to another game.

Uproar

Uproar refers to an argument in which two persons are locked in verbal combat, attacking each other, casting "you" statements back and forth:

> "You never do anything right!"
> "You are too compulsive."
> "You make my life miserable."
> "You're making mountains out of molehills."
> "You're playing favorites."

Anything can provoke an uproar: missing sales targets, errors, neglect, goofing off, the work environment, etc. But what happens is that the two parties involved slide back and forth between the Victim and the Persecutor poles, and the game ends with anger, frustration, and lots of bad feelings. The two parties involved hate each other's guts, distance themselves, and in many cases will engage in sabotage, guerilla warfare, or passive-aggressive revenge tactics. It is certainly a nonproductive pattern, and in marriages, when it is chronic, it is often the prelude to divorce. In work situations, after the game player has collected enough bad feelings, it often leads him or her to the exit door.

Win the Battle, Lose the War

This often happens to salespeople who are under pressure to hit a quota. Sometimes they will hard-sell a customer, and later the customer either has buyer's remorse or resents the pressure tactics and makes it a one-sale relationship. Sometimes the salesperson will practically give away the product at a ridiculous price, and then resent the customer's hardball negotiating tactics. Again this is picked up by the customer, and it becomes a one-sale relationship or, what is worse, a low price precedent is established with the customer that makes repeat business not even worth getting. Sometimes the salesperson may sell the customer a higher-priced product or a more sophisticated product that is vastly in excess of the customer's need, and this comes back to haunt the salesperson. In these cases the salesperson often feels victimized by management, and solves his or her problem by victimizing the customer. The payoff can be bad feelings all around, with resentment by the salesperson and resentment by the customer. The long-term payoff is that the salesperson is not welcomed back by the customer and has no chance of making this a customer for life because the canons of trust have been violated.

Sneakers

I call this game Sneakers because this is the first thing the salesperson puts on in the morning in order to prepare for the day. These salespeople typically book eighteen hours of work in a twelve-hour day, and are constantly running, always in a rush, always moving, always doing. Part of the problem is a problem saying no. These people live to please—to please their bosses; their spouses; their customers; their children; their coworkers. They have made a career out of rescuing everyone else. Someone comes up and says, "Would you attend this meeting for me? I just can't make it." The answer is yes. Another person says, "Would you serve on our Quality Committee?" Of course, the answer is yes. "Would you mind my cat this weekend? I'm going home to visit my sick father." Yes. "Would you change my order?" And so it goes: yes, yes, yes, yes . . . to everybody. What happens after a while is that these people are literally burdened down by obligations; they shuffle along with stooped shoulders, bearing the weight of all these folks imposing on them. Inside, the cry of the Victim is heard, "No one ever helps me. No one ever does anything for me. I'm always doing everything for everybody else. I'm fed up." Faced with this progressive buildup of pressure, the Victims seek release, and frequently they take one of two paths that give relief. One is that they slide to the Persecutor pole, and say in effect, "The next person who asks me for anything is going to get it." Then some poor innocent simply asks them something like, "Do you know where the telephone book is?" And the Victim blows up, becomes the Perse-cutor, and ventilates the bad feelings building up with an attack on the innocent who asked the question, saying, "What's the mat-ter with you, can't you find it yourself? You're always asking me for everything. I'm fed up with being the office's information booth." The innocent is left there with mouth flapping in the breeze, wondering what just happened. My experience is that when someone blows up at you out of all proportion to the stimu-lus you provided, that's a sure sign that it is not you; you were simply the last straw that broke the camel's back. What this does is to make Sneakers guilty, and sure enough, the way they get back into everybody's good graces is to say yes, yes, yes.

However, there is another path that many Sneakers use, and that is to get sick. The beauty of getting sick is that it legitmately can get you relieved of any responsibility whatsoever. If you do not want to make love on a given evening, all you have to plead is headache. If you do not want to go to work and face a difficult task, call in sick. Even a twenty-four-second case of the swine flu will do the trick. Sickness is the one excuse that our society recog-nizes as a reason for not doing anything. However, in the hands of game players, it is often the method of choice to get some relief from their troubles. Victims in the workplace periodically avail themselves of this tactic, and the interesting thing is that their sick-ness may not be feigned. It can be real. In fact, in many cases of folks using this excuse, their sickness is patterned—monthly, quar-terly, semiannually, or annually, they come down with something that gives them a respite. Further, in the act of being sick, they legitimately make a claim for others to help them, call them, visit them, or send them cards and flowers, and they extract from others wishes to get well. It is simply a great strategy because not only do they get relieved of their responsibilities, but they get a ton of strokes they would not normally get.

Sales Psychiatrist

This game comes about as a consequence of people's learning about games and the language above—the Victim, the Persecutor, and the Rescuer. They engage in a new game where they call every-body else on their games, e.g., "You're into YDU,YB." "Oh, you're starting Uproar." "You're doing your Victim number again." What they have learned is simply a new way to put people down. So instead of being a Persecutor by doing their typical negative, critical routine, they apply this new language to their need to put down others. Often, this game is prelude to Uproar.

How Not to Get Hooked Into Games

Since games hurt, result in bad feelings, lower productivity, and ripple through every other aspect of a person's life, it is important to know how not to go down this path. Remember, it takes two people to play a game. Let's find out what *you* can do about it.

1. *Avoid the Victim, Persecutor, Rescuer roles.* It is important to make a distinction between the Victim, Persecutor, and Rescuer in the gamey sense and the bona fide, legitimate experience of being a victim, persecutor, or rescuer. For example, coming from your office, if I walk out to my car and get mugged in the parking lot, I am a real, legitimate victim. On the other hand, if I walk out from your office to my car for the tenth time, and in the parking lot I get mugged for the tenth time, you have a distinct suspicion that I have a need to get mugged, and if there is one mugger in your town, I'll find him. In the second instance, you have a Victim, with a capital V; in the first instance, a legitimate victim, with a small v.

Take the Persecutor. There are times when you have a legitimate need to criticize someone, and you do. That can be a bona fide, legitimate act on your part and not a gamey expression at all. Further, our society empowers judges to be persecutors, and they are held in the highest esteem. Parents on occasion must wear the black hat, if they don't want to raise a barbarian. Managers are expected to hold their people accountable, inform them about their progress, and analyze lessons learned from a failure. Sometimes this is regarded as persecution by the game players, but it is a legitimate part of a manager's job to maintain standards and help sales reps to succeed in meeting those standards. All of these are legitimate persecutory behaviors. On the other hand, you surely know folks who are making a career out of criticism—from morning to night, nobody escapes their wrath. When this happens, it is clearly a game the person is into.

So reflect on your style. If you must criticize, use *when* and Mamie Taylor's questions. Put your criticism in the context of what will help the other be more successful, and tell the person that you do care about his or her success. Also, with those folks in your life from whom you want something, it is hardly ever enough to ask for it once. Good people forget, so build repetition and reminding into your approach, and don't resent having to do it. Finally, do not shrink from criticizing others constructively when it is appropriate. But always use standards of fairness as your point of comparison, such as targets, quotas, what the competition does, or industry standards. It takes your comments beyond the personal into objectivity.

There are many occupations with a rescuing orientation, such as nurse, teacher, doctor, or psychologist, and many roles have rescuing dimensions, such as parent, manager, or coach. These are all legitimate expressions of caring. Some people, however, like the ones who are into Sneakers, are preoccupied with rescuing others, even when they don't want to be rescued, and in more extreme cases these people will even make victims so that they can then rescue them.

Simply being aware of these games puts you into a position not to play. My advice here is to simply know what they are, and elect not to go down that path. As to being a victim, take responsibility for your life and feelings, and figure out what you can do about your problem. As to persecuting others, heed the advice above, and follow the guidance in Chapter 12 on communicating in a caring manner. If criticizing is a habitual problem for you, try this heroic exercise: Go through one day without making a condemning judgment of anyone or anything, then gradually thereafter, day by day, reduce your output of darts and daggers.

As to rescuing, instead of rushing in and helping out others, wait until you are asked for your help. Although this is a great guideline if you are prone to an overdeveloped nurturing orientation, do not abandon common sense. If someone at an adjacent table in a restaurant gets a piece of steak caught in the throat, and you know how to do the Heimlich maneuver, don't say, "Don said to wait until you are asked for help." Jump up and do the Heimlich.

2. *Become aware of the games in your life.* Reflect on the games you might be involved in. Once you understand the poles, the dynamics, the clues that you are into a game, and the hurtful payoffs, you are in a position to analyze any game. Once you are aware that you are involved in games, you are in a position to elect not to play. The fascinating thing about games is that they are not one-time chance events. Rather, they are patterned, and they happen with the same people in the same way over and over again, with the same kinds of bad feeling resulting. Things that are patterned are predictable; things that are predictable are controllable. You cannot prevent others from doing what they have a need to do, but you can control your reaction to it. So, in the quiet of the night, reflect on the games you are involved in and decide what you are going to do that will *not* support the game. Then, when the game event predictably occurs, implement your plan.

3. *Get into a problem-solving mode.* First of all, decide who owns the problem that is the focus of the game. If the other person owns the problem, then he or she owns the responsibility for finding a solution. Bite your tongue before you slip into the "Why don't you(s) . . ." Rather, ask questions like the following: "What are you going to do about your problem?" or "What options are available to you to solve your problem?" or "What have you done so far?" or "What have others done to solve a problem similar to yours?" or "If I had this problem, what would you advise me to do?" And if the person says to any of these, "I don't know," simply say, "Well, if you did know, what would you do?" This often catches game players completely off guard, and they start reciting possibilities. In any event, do not send solutions. In fact, you do *not* do them a favor when you do so. When you solve their problems, it teaches them not to think, and fosters a dependency relationship with you. Or they may just deep-six your suggestions, and then you will get angry. It's often helpful in impasses, where someone has a problem but no solutions and wants to dump it at your door, for you to say kindly, "Look, take some time out, generate a few options, and come back with what you think makes sense. Then we can evaluate it."

4. *Do what they least expect.* If someone into a persecutory mode attacks you, do just the opposite of what that person expects from you. Kiss the person, dance, twirl about, laugh, smile, but recognize that it is the other person who needs to be in the attack mode, and that you do not have to fall into the bad feeling trap. Incidentally, in your creativity, don't get caught up in a sexual harassment trajectory—use your common sense to interrupt their negativity. However, imagine a tug of war between two parties, pulling back and forth, each trying to get the other into a water-filled ditch. Put yourself in the picture. The other person throws the rope over for you to start. You grasp it, but when your opponent gives a mighty tug, you let go. Who has the problem? You have indicated that you are not going to play. That's what you can do by not playing a game. That's when you can leap across the ditch, lift the person up, dance, problem-solve, or listen to the problem.

5. *Reaffirm you own 10ness.* Games are a red herring. Game players adopt the Victim, Persecutor, or Rescuer orientation in order to escape reality and not deal with the real issues. Game players avoid problem solving, avoid using their own incredible creativity, and take the bad feeling way out that can destroy intimacy, affection, or a team experience. Ninety-nine times out of a hundred, game players are operating from a fear and terror mode rooted in the ache of their own fundamental sense of worthlessness. The self-worth at the core of a person's identity is clearly not at a 10 level, because 10s do not have a need to play games. Remember, the 2s are those who believe that they are less than a 10 in terms of their self-worth, and in their behavior with others they exhibit what they do to themselves. They are alienated from themselves, they hurt inside, they are afraid, they have not learned to celebrate themselves, and, as a consequence, they do not want anyone to get too close to them for fear that others will find out what they are really like. So games are the strategy of choice for people with a pitiful sense of their own self-worth. The dynamics of a game drive others away, alienate the parties, are nonproductive, and lead to bad feelings and estrangement. The game-playing strategy, although nonaware on the part of the game players, thus becomes self-fulfilling: Their worst fears about themselves get veri-

fied in their experience. They wind up alone, and are failures in creating a great life.

This is why for you the strategy of celebrating your own worth and selling yourself on yourself as your quintessential sale needs to be followed every day. Then, communicating in a caring manner lets you reach out to the game players and stay focused on the problem, and insulates you from the emotional smoke.

Summary and Bridge

Now you know what game playing is all about and some games found in your workplace. By applying the conceptual tools, you can recognize games wherever they occur—in your family, friendships, or wherever. You also know how to say no to games and avoid the incredible waste of energy that ripples through a person's experience when he or she does play games. Last, when you refuse to be a party to games, the other person knows that he or she has to be straight, deal with the problem, and be open, honest, and direct in order to have a fulfilling, productive relationship with you.

The next chapter goes beyond relationships and deals with the larger issue of solving problem in any arena.

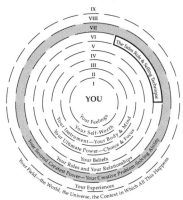

16

Problem Solving

	Yes	No
1. Would you like to know why problem solving is the antithesis of victimization?	☐	☐
2. Is it important for you to know how to jump-start your imagination?	☐	☐
3. Would you like to learn how to greet problems as friends and as opportunities?	☐	☐

About 100 years ago, a famous clergyman by the name of Russell Herman Conwell had a dream. His dream was to found a college for poor and deserving boys, but he had a problem—no money. To solve this problem, he began giving lectures. Over a thirty-nine-year period he gave 6,000 lectures, singlehandedly raising over $7,000,000 for his college. In every one of the lecturers, Dr. Conwell told a story entitled, "Acres of Diamonds." It was about an African farmer who had heard tales of other settlers who made millions by discovering diamond mines. When he heard these stories, he could hardly wait to sell his farm to the first interested buyer. He spent the rest of his life wandering the vast African continent, searching unsuccessfully for the diamonds that brought such high prices in the markets of the world. Finally, in a fit of despondency, broke and desperate, he threw himself into a river and drowned.

Meanwhile, one day, the man who had bought his farm found an unusual stone in a stream that cut a path through the property. It turned out to be a great diamond of enormous value. He then discovered that the farm was covered with them. It was to become one of the world's largest diamond mines.

The first farmer had owned literally acres of diamonds, but sold them for next to nothing in order to look for them elsewhere. If he had only taken the time to study and prepare himself, and learn what diamonds looked like in a rough state, and had first thoroughly explored the land he owned, he would have found the millions he sought right on his own property.

In a certain sense you and I are standing on an acre of diamonds. These acres of diamonds are our minds, our problem-solving capability. You and I know that great accomplishments start with ideas. Ideas are what make you grow, or a company grow, and in business, growth is the cutting edge for profit. If a company is not growing, it is already in decline. If you are not growing, you are already in decline. A crucial task for you and for me, therefore, is to have a plentiful supply of new ideas that point the way to doing things faster, more effectively, more productively, more profitably, and with more fun. A way to do this is to apply yourself to learning the techniques in this chapter and the next two chapters. They will increase your chances of growing better than most ways I am aware of.

Attitude to Bring to Problems

One thing you need to understand is that life is a problem crying out for a solution. Happiness is a problem crying out for a solution. Your sales quota is a problem crying out for a solution. Your family life is a problem crying out for a solution. Your religion, your philosophy, your lifestyle, your attitude, your relationships are all problems crying out for solutions. Problems are everywhere. How should I use my time tonight? Where should I eat? How much should I give? Where should I live, or take a vacation? How can I make more money? How can I take care of my health? How can I get to live the good life? How can I salt away enough for a good retirement? What should I do with my sick parent? How can I meet some interesting people? What should I wear tonight?

Problems are everywhere; in fact, to paraphrase Descartes, "I have a problem, therefore I exist." Problems go with the turf. Problems are an unrelenting fact of life. Actually, the day you and I have no problems is the day we will be into our final solution—death. So since problems are everywhere, should we curse the darkness, moan about our poverty, and decry our lost youth, or should we greet problems like a welcome guest? You know the answer. If you spend your time blaming and condemning there will be little left over to get on with life. Little problems get bigger, and past problems gobble up the present moment. In no time you are old, crusty, and sick.

So how do you approach problems? Accept that it is an imperfect world populated by mere mortals who are forever making mistakes or exercising poor judgment, and that having problems is part of the human condition. Approach problems pragmatically, staring stark reality in the eye, accepting problems as the natural order of things, and seeing them as an invitation to make something better, as an opportunity to improve and progress. This way not only are you *not* making a condemning judgment about your problem, you are, in fact, making a positive judgment. Positive judgments lead to good feelings, and good feelings thrust you right off into a problem-solving mode. Solving problems leads to action, and action leads to results. Results are what count.

The first thing to do when confronted with a problem is to put yourself into a problem-solving mode.

The Problem-Solving Mode

The problem-solving mode is the state of action. It is the state in which a person is moving ahead into the future, going after some goal. But the kinds of goals you go after depend on the kinds of questions you put to yourself. So what is the flow? Feelings, choices, colored by beliefs, questions, action, results. If you have put yourself into a state of enthusiasm, or feeling good, you are a potential waiting to be actualized; you are a reservoir of energy waiting to flow. What moves you in a given direction? It is the kind of questions you ask.

Let's take a worst-case scenario first. You are feeling bad, the bad feelings sap your energy level, you start experiencing waves of victimization and hopelessness, and you get flooded by more bad feelings. What kind of questions do you ask? Often folks in this nonachieving mode ask a type of not-real question. A not-real question, as the name implies, is really not a question, but a condemning judgment smuggled in under the grammatical guise of a question. It looks like a question and sounds like a question, and if you wrote it out on a piece of paper, an objective observer might even say it was a real question. How do you know it is not a real question? By the way it sounds, by the intonation in the voice, by the feelings of anguish melded into the expression. For example, a salesman who has just lost a sale asks himself, "Why does this always have to happen to me?" "What's the matter with me?" "Why do I always get the tough nuts?" These are *not* real questions searching for an answer; they are really condemning judgments— "It was not fair that I lost that sale"; "Something is wrong with me"; "That prospect was impossible and unreasonable." Remember what condemning judgments do. They open up the sluice gates to feelings—in the case above, feelings of inadequacy and feelings of anger. These feelings deepen a person's sense of powerlessness. But what provoked them? The not-real questions. The net effect of these questions is that they make it exceedingly difficult for the person to move out of the quagmire of negative feelings into a problem-solving mode. Heavy-duty negative feelings unleashed by condemning judgments lead a person to inaction; inaction leads to more of the same nonachieving state; and, as a further consequence, bad things tend to get worse. In worst-case scenarios, people develop depression and want to lie in bed all day long sucking their thumb with the covers over their head.

Okay, we know what not-real questions do, but what can real questions do? First, understand what a real question is. A real question is a thought expressing a desire on the part of the questioner to fill an information need that is not presently being filled. The correct answer or answers to a question are the pieces of a puzzle that, when accepted, give the questioner intellectual wholeness, satisfaction, harmony. The intellectual plausibility of the answer then becomes the springboard either for more questions or for a plan of action. The plan of action then motivates the person to action, and only with action will any results occur.

The beauty and power of real questions are that they signify hope, that there is a way, that there are possibilities out there. Real questions are by definition optimistic. They connote that there is light at the end of this tunnel. Questions stimulate and provoke; they are not accepting of the status quo. Questions are by nature subversive, and the first thing that occurs when you are living in a totalitarian society, or perhaps with a dictatorial boss or parent, is that you are not allowed to question authority. Why? Because by asking questions about something, you are, in that very act, suggesting that there might be another way to do something. That is subversive.

So what is part of the moral lesson here? Be subversive! Ask questions! Questions are the beginning of wisdom. Questions start the search for a better way. Real questions and the act of questioning are what unleash creativity and get a person into a problem-solving mode. The answers to questions result in invitations to action, to trying something new or different from what the questioner is presently doing.

What Kinds of Questions Does It Make Sense to Ask?

Obviously, real questions are the questions of choice, but what would they look like? Remember that back in grade school, you came across interrogatives: who, what, where, why, how, and when. These are your springboard to new ideas; however, they need to be linked with at least two other grammatical elements: a verb, a noun or pronoun, or an adjective. Take an object of inquiry, such as a book, and consider some of the many questions you could ask about it: What is a book? Who writes books? Why do books get written? When did books first come into existence? How does a book reach a book store? Where are books stored? What color are books? What size do they come in? What is the most famous book written? Why are books organized the way they are? You could go on and on just asking questions.

Let's take something more relevant to you, a question you could ask yourself that could generate some new possibilities for you: How can I surpass my sales quota? Here are a few additional questions you could ask that might help: Who else could I call on? How could I get a good referral? Where could I go to improve my connections? What could I learn (say, think, create, add, eliminate, copy, demonstrate, write, read, etc.)? Where could I go that would be helpful? When is really the best time to connect with prospects? When will I implement some of these new ideas? Why do I approach a prospect the way I do? How can I do it even better?

The key to asking questions is waiting for the answer. Getting an answer is the reason that we ask a question in the first place, but to make the process productive, ask–*wait*–answer, ask–*wait*–answer. The rule of thumb is: If you ask a lot of questions, you will get a lot of answers. Not all answers are of equal value, but having a lot of answers to choose from increases the probability of obtaining a good one. So one of the essential keys to creativity is to have a lot of questions that you ask on a routine basis when confronted with any problem. Below is an array of provocative questions that you can apply to any problem. I call them the solution generators.

The Solution Generators

What is the problem? Formulate every problem in terms of a question.

What would an ideal solution look like? The paradox of creativity, as in goal achieving, is that it is important to start at the end.

What obstacles stand in the way of the solution to this problem? About obstacles: Ask who, what, why, when, where, and how; and what can I do about removing them?

What resources do I have available? About resources: Ask who, what, where, why, when, and how.

What can I do differently? Ask what else, with whom, where, when, why, and how.

> As to *how different*, simply plug in adjectives—faster, bigger, smaller, slower, leaner, simpler, cheaper, wider, narrower, easier, clearer, louder, etc.—and make a question out of each one.

> And plug in an array of verbs to make a question of each one of them: What could I do, change, copy,

expose, conceal, eliminate, add, subtract, promote, reduce, enhance, slow down, divide, reorganize, re-schedule, reverse, customize, mass produce, im-prove, etc.

How have others solved this or similar problems? Ask about models of success—who, what, where, why, when, and how. And consider how you could adapt these to the solution of your problem.

What two or more things, if joined together, would make something new?

How would someone from Mars solve this problem? Or from another culture? Or how would a child solve it?

Do a series of what ifs—What if money were no obstacle? What if opportunity dried up—how would I create new ones? What if everybody beat my price?

What else?

Remember, these questions may not all exactly fit your problem. When that is the case, simply pass over the question and move to the next question using the earlier format, ask–*wait*–answer. Then capture each idea, or even thought fragment, that bubbles up to the surface, and make a list of them. Afterwards you can come back, evaluate them, modify any one of them, and eventually select the ones that make some sense.

Summary and Bridge

The point emphasized here is the incredible power of questions. Questions are the beginning of wisdom, creativity, and stimulating your imagination; they are the lever for finding solutions to difficult problems. Questioning is the key to getting on with business, and the prelude to action.

In the next chapter I will show you many other ways to generate ideas, and then how to plug the idea generation process into quantum leap thinking, which is a particularly powerful methodology for stimulating your creativity. Once you become enthusiastic about your problem-solving ability and can see your creativity explode, you will make a profound leap in your own sense of power. Ideas are what separate leaders from followers, the adventurers from the couch potatoes, great salespeople from slugs, and excellence from mediocrity.

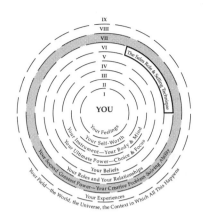

17

Nine Ways to Stimulate Your Creativity

	Yes	No
1. Is it important to you never to be at a loss for ideas?	☐	☐
2. Would you like to harness the incredible power of association?	☐	☐
3. Would you like to learn how to maximize your flow of ideas?	☐	☐

You do not have quota problems, finance problems, spouse problems, kid problems, career problems, or health problems. What you have is a lack of ideas problem. Or, to clarify this, what you lack is a variety of solutions to your problem from which to choose. If you have one solution to a complex problem, you are in a deficit situation. In fact, so often, when people have a profound problem, they go with the first solution that pops into their head. A rule of thumb in creativity is that if you have a lot of ideas, you increase the chances of getting a quality idea. Suppose, for example, you wanted to buy a nice ripe tomato. You walked into a supermarket, approached the tomato bin and found one tomato there. How would you feel? Suppose promoters were having a Mr. America/ Ms. America body beautiful contest, and you were the only person who showed up for the contest. How would the promoters feel? Suppose you were hungry, went to the buffet table, and found only one dish of pickled beets. How would you feel? The point here is simple: The best way to solve problems with quality ideas is to have a lot of ideas. In this chapter you will discover at least nine ways to tap your creative imagination and come up with a flood of possibilities to solve any problem.

Random Inspiration

The interesting thing about your brain is that you have filed away there billions of disconnected pieces of information; everything you ever read, saw, smelled, felt, heard, or experienced is recorded there. You have an incredible reservoir of potentially useful solutions. You just need to be able to access them and then put them together in the right combination. That's where idea stimulation comes in, and the incredible thing is that anything can stimulate a thought, an idea, or a solution. So how can you access this information randomly. Suppose my problem is: How can I improve my sales income by $50,000?

Make a list of seven concrete simple words, e.g.:

Grass
Bee
Mozart
Alarm
Noodle
Junk
Lamp

These words came out of my mind with no analysis, no premeditation, and no sense of how they might be useful. What's the principle? *Anything* can stimulate an idea. For each word, I ask myself, what might it suggest for solving the problem of improving my sales income by $50,000? I want you to notice the stream of consciousness, and note that every idea gets written down, even the wild, weird, bizarre ones. Why? Because they might suggest something else, or, when modified, might become great ideas.

Grass. Get a referral system that touches the grass roots, the lower-level people, for leads; make competitors green with envy by having an event with a celebrity; cover all possible prospects; have a grass skirt Hawaiian theme party for prospects; pay folks who give me leads that result in business; go to the watering holes of influentials.

Bee. Just spend my time on the prospects that are going to produce nectar and avoid the others; rest periodically to refocus; become a queen bee and find ways to get others to refer business to me; go where the prime prospects are--bees go where the flowers are; find out where prospects socialize, golf, exercise, etc. The best source of new business is old, satisfied customers—that's where the honey is.

Mozart. Have a musical event for prospects, and do a soft sell; put a marketing tape together combining beautiful music and my message; have a contest where listeners have to guess the correct musical piece, and get a reward; find out the type of music my customers prefer and build music into my presentations; become a little wacky like Mozart, and allow my eccentricity to become a door opener.

Alarm. Warn prospects of dangers they might fall into if they do not use my product; combine my product with a need to be safer from criminals; for every order, give a self-defense course; wake prospects up to the benefits of my product. No one is going to know about me or my product unless I send the alarm—do something larger than life that is attention-getting in a constructive sort of way.

Noodle. Create a dining event built around noodles; using a noodle as the image, give away free a creativity seminar where customers/prospects learn how to use their noodle; adopt flexibility as my hallmark—everything is negotiable, nothing is fixed; eat the competition's lunch; move into the Chinese market and other ethnic markets; dry noodles are brittle—put prospects into a survival soup; pitch message at customers' need to survive and grow.

Junk. One man's junk is another man's treasure; maybe there is a market for our used product or defective product; junk companies or failing companies are the ones most in need—target them; take junk business opportunities and figure out how to do profitable business with them—it would expand my range of prospects.

Lamp. Be a source of enlightenment for my prospects/customers; show them how to save money and increase productivity with my product; build a campaign around Aladdin's three wishes—get three wishes from a prospect and then show how my product can contribute to fulfilling each wish; don't hide my light under a bushel basket—promote, promote, promote. I have a great product that can lighten their load.

I used seven random words and in twenty minutes came up with twenty-eight ideas. Make no mistake, not all of the ideas are great. But what we are looking for is at least one good idea. If you run back over this list and start evaluating the ideas, you can see that there is more than one good idea. That's the goal—many ideas lead to a great idea.

Two Other Random Strategies

Since anything out here in the universe can stimulate a good idea, anything selected *randomly* from that universe has potential. However, to put some boundaries around it, try the telephone book Yellow Pages as a source of inspiration. Start paging through at random, asking yourself, "How can I improve my income by $50,000?" Industries, companies, words, possibilities, actions, will leap out at you. As they do, once again, write them down without any critique, and move on with some speed. In fifteen minutes you will have a range of ideas or idea fragments that you can play with, modify, and develop into something fruitful.

Another method of random selection is to use the Bible as your source. Believers use the Bible for finding divine guidance. Some do it by opening the Bible at random, closing their eyes and putting their index finger at a specific line. Then they read that passage, and feel that God is giving them special guidance for that day. You don't have to be a believer to use the Bible. You could even use the Koran, a Dr. Seuss book, a novel—any book! But, using the same method described above, write down the message and ask, "How can this help me increase my income by $50,000?" Listen to your inner voice and copy down your response. For example, with this problem in mind, I opened the Bible randomly, and this is the passage my index finger pointed to: Numbers 16:46—"and Moses said to Aaron, 'Take your fire pan, put live coals from the altar in it, and put some incense from the altar in it, and put some incense on the coals. Then hurry with it to the people and perform the ritual of purification for them. Hurry!' " Now, doing a stream of consciousness with my problem in mind, here are some possibilities: have a greater sense of urgency about what I am doing; take some hot prospects to our corporate altar to meet the CEO; identify my really hot prospects, and work with them, now; give my best customers a preview of products that are coming down the pike— give them the sense that they are insiders; develop some kind of strategy (ritual) that can get new prospects indebted to me, such as a survey, a problem-solving tool, a free seminar, or a meeting with a celebrity.

This process only took a few minutes. Read the passage, reflect on your problem, wait, listen, and then write down what comes to your mind; then go back and read all or a part of the passage and repeat the process again and again until you think you've about done it. Remember, all you need is one good idea, and anything can be a source of inspiration.

Other sources of random inspiration can be the newspapers, encyclopedias, directories of any sort, glossaries in the back of books, dictionaries, magazines, etc.

Two Random Words

Let's extend the notion of random words and make it a little more bizarre. In column A make a list of concrete words, and then in column B make another list. These lists can be as long as you want, but to give you the gist of the technique, I will use five, and then illustrate how three pairs can produce ideas you might never have thought of otherwise.

Column A	Column B
Radio	Bungee Cord
Waste Can	Wire
Mouse	Banana
Hair	Dog
Wheel	Flat

Once you have the two columns, draw a connecting line from any word in column A to any word in column B. Do this without thinking and without any premeditation:

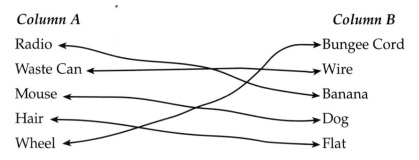

Now look at the pairs, and even reverse them: radio banana—banana radio; waste can wire—wire waste can; mouse dog—dog mouse; hair flat—flat hair; wheel bungee cord—bungee cord wheel. What do you do with these weird pairings? It's true that this exercise is a little more difficult than what you are generally used to and requires a suspension of your critical judgment, but go with it. Play with the pairings. You are looking for something that can help you solve your problem, i.e., improve your income by $50,000. Remember, anything can stimulate an idea! And once again, how many good ideas do you need? You're right—just *one!*

Take a look:

Radio Banana—Put commercials on the air that make people go bananas.

Banana Radio—Think about commercials to Costa Rica—Hispanic market.

Waste Can Wire—Send telegrams to waste remediation companies.
Wire Waste Cans—Send out miniature wire waste cans to tell prospects they can dump their problems there if they contact you.

Mouse Dog—Be dogged, persevering, in helping a company get rid of problems.
Dog Mouse—A mouse might bite a dog's tail; some problems interfere with a company's mission—give the solutions away and then sell your product.

Granted, these thoughts may not be of Nobel Prize character, but remember, what do you need? One good idea. Test it out.

Analogy

Using analogies is a productive way to generate ideas that might not have come to you if you simply used the left side of your brain, the logical, analytic, rational part. Imagination and insight often come out of the blue and can be triggered by the strangest, weirdest, wildest stimuli. That's why analogy can be so productive. An analogy is basically a comparison of likeness between two things. The easiest analogy to work with is a simile, which is a comparison overtly expressed, with *like* or *as* connecting the two elements compared; for example, making $50,000 more income is *like* pulling teeth, making $50,000 more income is *like* trying to harness lightning, making $50,000 more income is *like* drilling for oil in the ocean. In each of these instances, the comparison is plausible, and comparisons like these can often provoke interesting insights that can be helpful in solving a problem. But what I have discovered to be a more provocative source of creative stimulation is an implausible analogy, where the things compared have no obvious connection and might even seem ridiculous; for example, making $50,000 more income is *like* listening to country-and-western music; making $50,000 more income is *like* rollerblading; making $50,000 more income is *like* the Leaning Tower of Pisa.

Now, how do you use an implausible analogy to stimulate ideas? Make a list of the attributes of the thing to which your $50,000 problem is compared. For example, take the Leaning Tower of Pisa.

Attributes: It's tall; it's beautiful; it might fall; engineers have not succeeded in straightening it; tourists used to walk up it; it's old; it's built on a soft foundation; it's artistic; it's an attraction; it's unsafe.

With your $50,000 problem in mind, ask yourself what each one of these attributes might suggest that could help you solve your problem: I need something to make me and my product stand above the competition; point out the dangers if my prospects don't change to my product; build a long-lived, firm relationship with my customers; avoid the quick fix, the low price; build solid value and sell the long-term benefits; point out the beauty, artistry, elegance, and quality of my product; have a "take a walk with me sales call"—do business and become more fit at the same time; compare prospects' present way of doing business to the Leaning Tower; compare the competition's product to the Leaning Tower—a catastrophe waiting to happen.

That's the idea. The attributes operate like a list of random words. They are provocative, and they can help you reach into your incredible data bank and pull out something that makes sense.

Empathetic Creativity

What this means is to get out of yourself and become the other. If you look at the world only from your own perspective, you are very narrowly constrained in terms of unearthing a multiplicity of possibilities for solving your problem. Suppose your problem is improving your income by $50,000. Try analyzing your problem by being a customer who does not have a perceived need for your product. Become that customer; enter that customer's skin; see the world from that customer's viewpoint; look at the world in terms of the needs that customer has—the pressures, the constraints, the fears, the concerns, the career, and of course, how the customer perceives you. Once you start seeing the world the customer's way, the objections he or she might have will become apparent, and the opportunities that exist will become more apparent. This exercise requires a leap of imagination. You are becoming an actor, yet while you are acting, you are also analyzing and capturing in writing the things that might shed some light on your problem.

Here is another list of other persons and things to be:

- A customer who does have a problem—and needs to solve it
- The secretary of a customer
- Your product
- Your boss
- The competition
- The economy
- The customer's boss

Try it out, and you will be surprised how fruitful it can be to give you a keener insight into others, your product, your service, the competition, etc.

Show Childlike Inquisitiveness

The favorite word of a little boy or girl is *why*. "Why does grass grow, Daddy?" "Why is grass green, Mommy?" "Why do we have grass?" "Why do people cut grass?" "Why do people plant grass?" "Why does grass turn brown sometimes?" "Why . . . why . . . why . . . ?" *Why* is a magical word because it is so provocative. It forces the person to whom it is addressed to think. One technique that is particularly fruitful in generating insight into any problem, any solution, or anything is to string the whys in a row, just as a little child would do, to try to achieve full understanding. Take, for example, the problem we have been working with of improving your income by $50,000.

Q. Why are you not already achieving it?
A. Because I have not been making enough sales.
Q. Why are you not making enough sales?
A. Because I do not know who would want my product.

Q. Why don't you know who would want your product?
A. Because they are not telling me that they do.
Q. Why don't they tell you that they do need your product?
A. Because they don't know me.
Q. Why don't they know you?
A. Because I have never met them.
Q. Why don't you meet them?
A. Because I haven't taken the steps to put myself in a position to do so.
Q. Why not?
A. No good reason.

Aha! Maybe if I developed a plan to meet good prospects informally, outside of business, in a relaxed atmosphere, I could make some viable connections. I could join a golf club or an athletic club, get on the board of the local museum, maybe become a member of the local Chamber of Commerce or Rotary, join a yacht club or sailing club, or perhaps a wine tasting club or gourmet cuisine organization. Any of these could improve my network of good connections.

Asking why is like peeling an onion, and it is a sure way to get to the bottom of a problem. In fact, it can help you clarify what your problem really is, and in the process even suggest some solutions you might not have otherwise thought of.

Mind Maps

My all-time favorite for doing almost anything is to start with a "dump." A dump is simply an outpouring of possibilities in response to a question. However, the best way to display the output is not as a list or in paragraph form, but in the form of a mind map. The reason why a mind map is so useful is that because of the very way it looks, other associations and ideas come to mind, stimulated by what you have already laid out, in a very ready manner. What does a mind map look like? First, let me describe the mind-mapping process. Get a blank piece of paper. At the top, write out the problem in the form of a question. Then, in the center of the paper, briefly write down your problem, using key words with a big question mark after them, and put a circle around the words and question mark. As concepts come to mind in response to the question in the center, put down their key word, put a circle around it, and attach a string to it leading back to the circle in the center. If ideas come from the categories you put up, as offshoots or subcategories, circle each one of them and attach a string to it leading back to the parent category. Since one picture of a mind map is worth many explicatory words, look at Figure 4.

Then, once the dump is out, you can develop an outline, select the ideas that make sense, or prioritize—it all depends on what your problem is. You can use it for anything: as a first step in devel-

Figure 4. Sample mind map.

Problem: How to convert dissatisfied customers into satisfied customers?

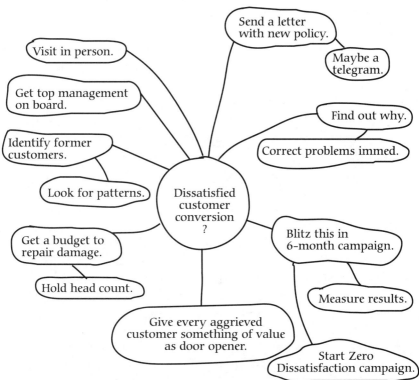

oping a speech you might have to give; as a display of all the things you might have to do in a given day; as a display of possibilities for resolving a problem and the prelude to the outline of a plan, as above; as a method of dealing with stress (e.g., put in the center, "What's bugging me?" and the simple outpouring of categories will make the stressed person feel better); or as a brainstorming tool to get an array of ideas out there without worrying about order, correctness, or evaluation. I am such a believer in its efficacy that before I write one word in a chapter, I do a mind map of the things I want to cover—invariably the things I put in the balloons suggest other things.

Environments for Creativity

Right now, as I am typing this sentence, I am listening to a CD that, strangely, in May 1994 hit the top of the pop charts in sales. It is called *Chant*. It has nineteen chants sung by the Benedictine monks of Santo Domingo de Silos, Spain. What I discovered is that the slow movements of the chants are tranquilizing, and make me twice as productive as I normally am. Music is like that, and the slow movements of symphonies, particularly Baroque ones, can do the same thing for your creative disposition as the chants. The moral of this is not to make you a monk, but to remind you of the power of music to help you in your problem-solving efforts.

Tranquility is great for supporting creativity. Listening to water falling, like from a fountain in a Japanese rock garden, does just that. Sounds of nature from your CD also are pacifying.

Breathing fresh air is also a tonic. If you are working in a hermetically sealed building, just go outside and take a few deep diaphragmatic breaths, and you will be completely reenergized.

The colors you look at make a difference to your energy level and tranquility. For example, in many police stations, walls are painted pink. The police have discovered that thugs, muggers, burglars, and murderers are easier to handle in that kind of environment than with walls painted almost any other color.

Work standing up at an elevated desk periodically. If your brain turns to marshmallow, take a break. It's the quickest way to get renewed. Being cemented into one type of seating position will give your brain "carpal tunnel syndrome." Move around.

If you really need to get reinvigorated, take a brisk walk, jog, or take a shower and end it with cold water, gradually lowering the temperature until you can't stand it anymore. You'll feel like a new person.

Put beautiful pictures on your walls. When you gaze on them, they will raise your energy level. Also, keep a book of poetry handy. When you are stuck or need a break or inspiration, simply open your book of poems and read aloud. You'll feel the difference immediately.

Finally, do your MRE (mental renewal exercise). I have found that one of the times I get my greatest flashes of insight is when I am doing my MRE. When you are done with a given MRE, after you have had an inspiration, immediately write it down so that you won't forget it. Further, you will find that when you do MRE on a regular basis, as I suggested earlier, on top of everything else good that happens, your creativity will simply explode.

Summary and Bridge

This chapter is an encouragement to say yes to using some exercises that can help enhance your problem-solving ability. Each one of these exercises can send up positive ripples that affect every other area of life, because using them is an affirmation of hope that there is a way—a better way. Since life is all about solving problems, ability in this department is a powerful catalyst to greater sales and a greater life.

The next chapter deals with a technique that can particularly help successful salespeople who, as part of their reward for achievement, get their next year's quota ratcheted up.

18

Quantum Leap Thinking

	Yes	No
1. Would you like to discover how to make your sales quota seem easy?	☐	☐
2. Would you like to master a strategy that can springboard you into the star category?	☐	☐
3. Would you like to discover a new and exciting way to solve all your problems?	☐	☐

Quantum leap thinking is a simple method to stimulate you to create. It is a method that prompts you to stretch your imagination and come up with a unique idea that could lead *possibly* to a quantum leap, and *definitely* to the achievement of your goals. It forces you to break out of the habit of nonthinking and of dozing in the comfort of routine—"the way we have always done it." It challenges you to tap your most unused natural resource—your imagination.

Scientists tell us that most of us do not use more than 10 percent of our brain power. Research has shown us that most people barely use the right side of the brain. The left side of the brain is what has been emphasized and rewarded in our education and in most businesses. That is the part of the brain that reasons; that is logical, analytical, and judgmental; that plans and evaluates; that seeks for the one solution, deals in proof, and has a need to be right all the time. It is an extremely important part of the mind, but the other side is our acre of diamonds that is hardly mined. It is the right side that is the source of creativity, insight, intuition; the part of us that pictures and visualizes; the part of us that generates ideas, rearranges phenomena, helps us break out of cliché patterns, and sees things in a wholistic sense. It is also the part of us that works while we sleep and that can work even while the left side is preoccupied with other concerns. Most employees do not know how to mine that acre of diamonds. Some of the guidance given earlier helps, but quantum leap thinking puts all the creative stimulation and idea generation into a context that magnifies the possibilities for innovation immensely. It is part of a method to generate that quantum leap contribution by mining the right side of the brain and wedding it with the left.

The Method

Quantum leap thinking has seven steps:

1. Establish a baseline goal.
2. Escalate the baseline goal to a quantum leap goal.
3. Take ownership of the quantum leap goal.
4. Invent ways to achieve the quantum leap goal.
5. Select high-yield ideas.
6. Incorporate high-yield ideas into a baseline plan of action.
7. Do it!

Sales Example

Suppose that you are in sales and your boss has just handed you your annual sales quota: $1 million. Last year was a great year for you, but in sales, part of the perverse reward of success is that the annual sales target keeps getting ratcheted up. This year your boss raised it by 10 percent. She said, "You can do it." An increase by

10 percent from one year to the next may not seem to be much, but if you think about it, at a 10 percent increase a year, after seven years the target will be almost double, or $2 million. This target often causes great stress to salespeople. They get burned out, get sick more often, and use more anesthetics to kill the pain, such as drink, smoking, or drugs. Why? Because the overwhelming majority use the same selling method in going after $2 million as they did seven years ago going after $1 million. What's the consequence? Many of the high achievers wind up working seven days a week, ten or more hours a day, and their personal and family life suffers. Others hit their comfort zone and plateau out. They have decided that a certain number, such as $1.7 million is their number, and despite all the gyrations of the sales manager, that's all they are going to do. All of these folks are prime candidates for quantum leap thinking.

Suppose your target is $1 million in sales. Make a quantum leap goal out of it by putting it on a grander scale. In this instance, since the target is readily quantifiable, multiply the baseline goal by 10. The quantum leap goal is thus not $1 million, but $10 million.

Now notice step three in quantum leap thinking: "Take ownership of your quantum leap goal." What this means is that you make believe that your sales target for this next year is $10 million. It is absolutely necessary here, if you really want to reap the benefits of this method, to resist the impluse to say, "This is ridiculous. This is stupid. This doesn't make any sense whatsoever." Do not make any negative condemning judgment about the $10 million. Make believe that your life depends on achieving it, that the quality of your lifestyle depends on it, that your children's future depends on it, that the respect and esteem of the people you care for depends on it. Make believe that you do, indeed, have to make it happen. Again, please suspend your disbelief and accept it.

While you are taking ownership of your quantum leap goal of $10 million, ask yourself this one question: In the entire scheme of the universe, is it *possible* for you to hit that target? The answer to this question is yes! It is absolutely without a doubt *possible* for you to hit it.

Now look at step four. Invent ways to achieve your quantum leap goal. It becomes very apparent very fast that your present methodology for achieving your typical sales baseline target will *never* get you to your quantum leap goal. So the pursuit of your quantum leap goal forces you to invent some new strategies that will do it. The idea generation techniques described earlier can now be profoundly fruitful for you because the goal to be achieved or the problem to be solved will point the direction for your idea flow. So, recall for a minute the techniques discussed earlier:

- Questions, questions, questions
- Random words
- Random columns
- The Bible method, Yellow Pages, and other sources of stimulation
- Analogy—plausible and implausible
- Empathetic creativity
- Childlike inquisitiveness
- Mind mapping
- Environments for creativity—music, color, sounds of nature, breathing, water, movement, breaks, poetry, and MRE

Using any or all of these exercises in pursuit of ways to hit your quantum leap goal will pay off big for you.

Step five is to select high-yield ideas. Using the exercises above in the context of quantum leap thinking, you will generate a plethora of ideas. What you do here is go over your list of ideas and circle the ones that have particular merit. Two things can happen in this process; one is possible, and one is likely. By thinking about how to make a quantum leap, you might indeed find a way to make that quantum leap; for example, you might discover an entirely new market niche, a new application of your product, a new way to market your product, or even a new industry—some new way to, in fact, achieve your quantum leap goal. For sure, you will never discover a quantum leap idea if you never think about making a quantum leap. A quantum leap idea is *possible*, but it is *likely* that you will unearth a large number of high-yield ideas that you would never have thought of otherwise. This is really the payoff you are looking for because it is going to make your life more civilized immediately.

This leads to step six, which is to incorporate the high-yield ideas into your plan of action to achieve your baseline goal. Here you get back to reality and your task at hand, which is to hit your baseline target of $1 million. But you have just spent half a day or a day thinking of ways to achieve $10 million, and you are armed with many, many new ways to hit that baseline target. Further, after you have expended a lot of creative energy going after ways to hit $10 million, the task of hitting your baseline goal will seem easy. It will no longer be the stress generator, the source of irritation that it usually is, because now you have ideas that will enable you to work smarter.

Once you lay out your plan of action in steps that follow this formula, "to do how much of what by when," the last step is to *do it.* Nothing happens without action. And great things can happen when you have have great ideas that tell you what to do.

Applications

Sales managers would be well advised, when they give out annual quotas, to arm their salespeople with this methodology and allocate a whole day to the process. It would be a terrific investment in morale, and would increase the probability of every salesperson's hitting the targets. And institutionalize the process—do it every year.

If you are in sales and your manager is not enlightened enough to do quantum leap thinkiing, then do it on your own. You do not necessarily need the group stimulation. The payoffs are the same, and you can do the idea generation at your own pace.

The same methodology of quantum leap thinking can be applied to any problem you are working through. It's easy to escalate the baseline goal to a quantum leap goal if the baseline goal is readily quantifiable—just multiply it by 10. If doing that makes the quantum leap goal nonsensical, or if the baseline goal is not readily quantifiable, simply put the baseline goal on a grander scale. It is important that the quantum leap goal be a real stretch, a real quantum leap, way beyond the ordinary, not just a modest advance over the baseline goal. For example, suppose you have already reduced the cost of your product to bare bones, and you have a baseline goal of reducing it 10 percent more. If you take 10 times that as your quantum leap goal, that would reduce the cost to 0, and that is truly ridiculous. To make it a quantum leap goal, put the cost-cutting effort on a grand scale—invent a cost-cutting methodology that brings national renown to the department, become a corporatewide model for cost cutting and a training center for other departments, become the cost-cutting benchmark department for the entire industry, etc.

Summary and Bridge

Quantum leap thinking is a giant yes! to your creative imagination. It creates a context in which achievement of a baseline goal is a piece of cake, but it holds out the possibility that you might invent a quantum leap. Doing quantum leap thinking is fun, it is energizing, and as an add-on to your problem-solving capability, it can send positive ripples into every quarter of your life.

The next chapter provides some guidance about what you can do with all these great ideas you discover and, eventually, how to move into action.

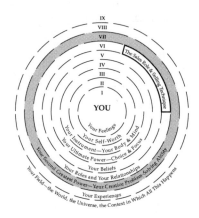

19

Ideas, Filters, Decisions, and Plans

	Yes	No
1. Is it important to you to be more effective in your execution?	☐	☐
2. Would you like to learn how to separate the forest from the trees?	☐	☐
3. Would you like to know how to create a plan of action that has teeth in it?	☐	☐

Let us assume, for the sake of discussion, that you have questioned, visualized, quantum leaped, and used a variety of idea generation exercises in an attempt to solve a problem that is important to you. If you followed instructions, you now have a laundry list with a plethora of possibilities, some of which are fragmentary, some obvious, some ingenious, and some in need of development and modification. Play with this list and circle the ideas that at first glance appear to have merit.

When you step back, you will notice that the ideas you have circled are not all of equal value. In order to determine the ones that you are going to use, it is necessary to evaluate the ideas, and there are a number of ways to do this. The first way is to simply list the ideas in order of merit—the idea that has the highest potential, the next, the third, the fourth, etc. Establishing priorities or levels of importance or potential is a routine to get into whenever you have a variety of possibilities to choose from.

Another way to evaluate the merit of an idea is to look at it against the following criteria: risk, investment, effectiveness, ease, and feel.

Risk

By risk I mean what is the worst thing that could happen if you did use the idea and the idea went down the drain? Here I am referring to the cost of failure. It is important to be optimistic and positive, but to avoid being a Pollyanna, it is always wise to consider a worst-case scenario when a future course of action is involved. Why? Because things do not always work out as expected; you do not get the results expected, or the assumptions you made were faulty, or the conditions change, or things beyond your control entered into the equation.

Anticipating what might go wrong, and what you could do if it did, can in itself be a creative exercise and can generate a remedial plan or damage control ideas that make the step worth trying. The other important aspect of analyzing risk is that it allows you to ask the question mentioned earlier, which, when coupled with an analysis of the cost of failure, can give you a go/no-go signal—could I live with that worst possible outcome? Thus, if the idea has high-level potential, and your answer to the second question is yes! then do it. If your answer is no, then you'd better not bet the farm on it. The risk/reward ratio is just not worth it.

Suppose one of your ideas to improve your income was to get a list of the presidents of all the companies in your county and call them, with an eye to getting an appointment. In the past you discovered that entering an organization somewhere at the bottom of the hierarchy or at the middle level resulted in a lot of delay and few successes. You think calling the president might be more productive. Using the risk criterion, you ask yourself, "If I called the president of a company for an appointment, what is the worst thing that could happen?" Well, you conclude that the worst thing that could happen is that the president says no to an appointment. Since you do not now have an appointment with a president, a no means simply that your present situation has not changed. Could you live with that no? You reflect that you are already living without that appointment, so you could certainly continue to live without it. On the other hand, you say, "I might get a yes." That yes would advance you in your sell cycle. Further, it is also quite possible that even if the president said no, he or she could refer you to the person who would be the right one to deal with. Calling that person after being referred by the president increases the likelihood of getting an appointment with him or her by about 80 percent. It's clear from this quick analysis that the risk attached to this strategy is negligible. So, on this criterion you have a green light. Now it is useful to look at the idea using the other four criteria.

Investment

Investment is what you put into an action. Investment is usually looked at in terms of money, and in business most things can be given a dollar value. Some good ideas are free, such as changing the way you think about yourself, eating properly, planning better, improving your relationships. In fact, most of the ideas suggested in this book require a minimal dollar investment. They do require an investment of time, energy, and focus, but you do not have to spend two hundred dollars on tapes, or come to my knowledge spa, or buy my hotline (all of which I don't have, incidentally). However, as you run through your list of ideas, consider the investment involved. Is it low or high—a small amount or a large amount? Ideally, you are looking for a high-yield idea that requires only a small investment. But don't scratch an idea just because it requires a large investment. What this criterion does is to make the issue apparent, and it's better to know in advance what something is going to cost.

To go back to the idea of calling company presidents in your county for an appointment, what is the investment? Basically, it is your time. Suppose your sell cycle typically starts with you picking up the phone and cold-calling prospects to get an appointment. Well, since you already have to call somebody, calling presidents does not, in fact, require any additional investment. You conclude that since the probabilities of success are decent and the risk is negligible, this idea gets a green light on investment.

Effectiveness

This criterion answers the question: Will it do the job? Is it the hammer to hit the nail? Is it the right size wrench to turn the nut? I regularly get calls from the telephone company suggesting that I put my company's name in the Yellow Pages and take an ad to announce to the world my capabilities and services. After twenty years in the consulting business, and having followed their advice for a number of years, I have discovered that this is a totally ineffective form of business promotion for me. Why? In my business—seminars/consulting—word of mouth, cold calling, and giving talks are the ways in which I have gotten 99 percent of my business. The only time anyone who used the Yellow Pages has called me was when the person was looking for a job.

So, reflect on whether this action will help get you the result you want. If it is a nice blue-sky thought but it won't get you the results you want, toss it overboard. If it is an effective idea, the risk is absorbable, and the investment low or tolerable, then move to the next criterion.

In the case of cold-calling company presidents, you conclude that it is indeed an effective path to test out. One, you might get an appointment; two, you might get a good referral; three, the risk attached to the calls is zero; four, it does not require any additional investment in time and effort. This brings us to the fourth criterion.

Ease

This is just a shorthand way to consider the ease of implementation of an idea. Some ideas can be implemented immediately, and are under your control. All they require is a decision to do them, and you do them. On the other hand, some ideas require a long period of development, sign-offs at many levels, and a reliance on others to supply crucial inputs at critical times. I am not saying that you should never undertake anything that is not easy to implement, but I am saying that when the swamp is filled with alligators snapping at your butt, you may not be around long enough to drain the swamp. Anything big, monumental, or of great significance is by nature a complex proposition, and often not easy to implement. Yet by overcoming the obstacles, great things can happen. So a balance needs to be maintained between ease and complexity. However, in the short term, steps that are high-yield and easy to implement are preferable over steps that are high-yield and complex.

Related to this concept is the element of reversibility. Occasionally you might be troubling over a decision to do something or not. Here is a rule of thumb that can help you be a man or woman of action: If an action step is high-yield and, if taken, is reversible, do it immediately. If an action step is high-yield but is not reversible easily, then before you do it, study it from every side, get opinions from people you respect, and sleep on it. For example, if you are wondering whether to hire a sales assistant on a temporary basis, if the idea does not pan out, you can let the person go like that. On the other hand, suppose you want to terminate a full-time employee, and you do; that is pretty much an irreversible decision, one that would be profoundly difficult to undo if it was a bad move. Likewise, if you had a one-sale customer, you could give that customer 50 percent off, and if it turned out not to be a good idea, then the next customer who came through the door might only get 10 percent off. On the other hand, if you were looking to build a lifetime relationship with a customer over many sales, if you gave the customer 50 percent off and it turned out to be a bad move, you can be sure that it would be exceedingly difficult to try to lower that discount from the 50 percent level without losing the customer. The former decision was reversible, the latter irreversible. So the rule of thumb is to make reversible decisions fast and irreversible ones slowly—after you have done a thorough analysis.

To go back to cold-calling presidents in your county, is this step easy to implement or difficult? On reflection, you conclude that the only thing you need is an up-to-date list of these presidents, and that you can buy the business directory from your local

Chamber of Commerce for six dollars. Since this idea is high-yield, passes muster on the other three criteria, and is easy to acquire, the idea gets another endorsement, and that brings us to the final criterion to help determine the merits of an idea.

Feel

Here I am talking about a criterion that is hard to quantify, hard to demonstrate, and hard to prove. Sometimes, in the absence of clear proof, we get a gut feeling about the rightness or wrongness of a course of action. Your inner voice is saying yes or no to doing it. That inner voice is your intuition. Sometimes it is a strong hunch, and it always has a strong feeling component to it. That is why I summarize this criterion in one word, *feel.*

The big question is, how can you know whether your intuition is right or wrong, on target or way off? There are two ways. First, take a look at your history of intuition, your track record on hunches. In the past, when you got a hunch in advance, what was your batting average when you followed it? Was it high? If it turns out on examination that the predictive value of your hunches was pitiful, then until you develop your intuitive ability, stick to a more rational analysis by using the other four criteria—risk, investment, ease, effectiveness—and you will be on safe ground. On the other hand, if your intuition is usually on target, then when you combine it with the other four criteria, and your inner voice is saying "go for it," do it.

Many people have a great intuitive sense, yet they have a history of not listening to their inner voice. When they look at things in retrospect, they have found themselves saying, "Why didn't I follow my intuition?" If that is you, make it a policy to start relying on your intuition by first listening to your inner voice, and then, in low-risk arenas, following it. Gradually you will build up confidence in your intuition, and when you add "the feel" to the four choice criteria in your equation, you will have a powerful forward thrust to your life path.

As to cold-calling presidents of companies in your county, what does your inner voice say? How do you feel about the idea?

What does it say? Yes? No? You decide using the guidance suggested above.

Precision—Putting Teeth Into an Idea

Let us suppose that you have an array of high-yield ideas that can help you achieve your goal. Each idea needs to be cast in a format that is specific, precise, and measurable, and that has a deadline attached to it. Why? Because to make things happen in life, you need action ideas; nothing happens unless you take action. So each idea needs to be honed down to an action idea. The format that every idea needs to be translated into is: To do how much of what by when. When an idea follows that format, you have an action step. For example, on cold-calling presidents of companies in your county, how do you give it teeth? Following the do-how-much-of-what-by-when format, what would it look like? "Telephone 20 presidents a day." Or if you were a sales manager, with another concern, "Hire four new salespeople by the end of the first quarter." Or, "Sell 4,000 chairs by the end of the year." In each instance, the idea has an action, a measurable indicator, and a deadline. In every instance you would know what it would look like if it happened.

What Next?

Okay, let us suppose you have circled the ideas with merit, run them through the five criteria above, and given them teeth. What is necessary to make a plan? But first, why is a plan necessary? Because, to quote Robert Schuller, "If you do not have a plan, you have a plan to fail." Good things do not happen to people on a consistent basis if they do not create a plan to make them happen. Planning involves a goal, something you do not now have, but want to make happen sometime in the future. Goals are what can make a person come alive, give a person motivation, stimulate enthusiasm. Show me someone who is suffering from ennui and lassitude, is dissipated, disconnected, and unhappy, and is without drive and enthusiasm, and I will show you a person who does not have specific goals.

The paradox of goal setting is that it is necessary to start at the end. This means that you need to be able to recognize a goal if it happens. The best kinds of goals are the ones, like the action ideas, that you can measure, because at any given time you know exactly where you are, how far you have to go, and what you have to do to get there. That is the beauty of sales; not only is the end target measurable, but most of the things it is essential to do to hit that quota are also measurable.

Below I am going to propose a plan for a salesperson. You can use it as a model to tweak or modify for your own purposes. The explanations will be put in italics.

Salesperson Plan

Goal: To achieve $1 million in sales by the end of the year.
This is the final end result to be accomplished. It is specific, it is measurable, it has a deadline, and there is no ambiguity or vagueness about it at all.

Action Steps

Below are the steps it is necessary to take in order to achieve the goal above. They can vary depending on the type of selling you do. This example is for an outside salesperson. Notice how each action step is formatted in the do-how-much-of-what-by-when manner.

> *Prospecting*—Spend one-half day a week adding to and purifying my list, and selecting names from it to call during the following week.
> *Cold Calling*—Each day call twenty prospects on my list to make an appointment.
> *Appointments*—Call on three prospects a day.
> *Referrals*—From each appointment, obtain two referrals.
> *Presentations/Proposals*—Present/propose at least twice a week.
> *Follow-up*—Track all leads, referrals, deadlines as they develop by maintaining a current tickler file—ongoing.

Records—Spend one-half day a week maintaining accurate call
    reports, forecasts, and sales records.
Professional Growth—Take at least one advanced computer
    course to manage the sales task by year-end.
Read two sales technique books by end of year.

If a salesperson did all the things delineated in the action
steps, his or her likelihood of achieving $1 million would be excel-
lent. It really is simple. Do the right things, and you will get the
right results.

To make the above one-page plan graphic, you can actually
plot your progress against the plan, as shown in Figure 5, and one
picture then will be worth more than a thousand words.

It is equally desirable to plot your progress on each of the key
action steps. One way to do it in a uniform manner, so that you
can see a trend developing, is to get yourself a pad of graph paper
and plot *each action step,* as well as your overall end result sales
goal (see Figure 6). I recommend that you do this plotting at least
once a week.

In my judgment, you cannot overestimate the power of a
graphic picture to show you exactly where you are. It points out
trends that are unmistakable. My feeling is that this is honest selling. You know for sure exactly what you are doing or not doing.

Figure 5. Goal: Achieve $1 million in sales by year–end.

Amount of Sales		Jan.	Feb.	Mar.	Apr.	May	Jun.	Jul.	Aug.	Sept.	Oct.	Nov.	Dec.
	$1,000,000												
	900,000												
	800,000												
	700,000												
	600,000												
	500,000												
	400,000												
	300,000												
	200,000												
	100,000												
	0												

Month

Figure 6. Plot of cold calls on a weekly basis.

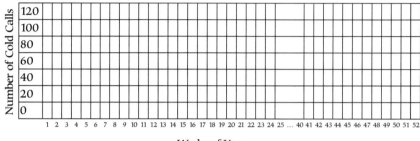

The disadvantage of this graphic accounting is that it makes your behavior leap out; there is no place to hide from the numbers and the picture they generate.

Doing Basic Selling

A graph highlights vividly whether you are doing the basics. Doing the basics in a regular manner is the way to do consistent good selling that will move you into the star category. What some salespeople will tell you is that these basic action steps take too much time. The fact is that if you did them, and measured how well you did them, you would obtain all the feedback you needed to determine whether you are doing enough to achieve your goal. Selling is simple, but what I have observed is that most salespeople do not do on a consistent basis what they learned in Salesmanship 101. By getting back to basics, plotting your progress, and using the feedback to correct your behavior, you are beyond impressions, going with the flow, resting on your laurels, or living in your comfort zone. When the basics are supported by quantum leap thinking, the path to excellence and beyond is achievable.

Summary and Bridge

This is a clarion call to do what you already know how to do: make yourself a plan following the to-do-much-of-what-by-when format, execute it as planned, and plot your results. Selling is not rocket science. Anyone with average intelligence and a pleasing personality who does the basics can be successful at it. The reason why so many salespeople are in so much trouble is that they, once again, do not do half of what they already know how to do.

A bit of advice not mentioned above for a sales manager is this: Teach your charges this simple planning technique, and require every salesperson to plot his or her progress on each action step. This will give you the basis for an informed coaching session. Any salesperson who is hitting his or her numbers on a regular basis can be left alone; with those who are not, you can then go into the details of their accounts and work habits. This is informed managing by exception.

The next chapter takes the big picture and longer-range goals and makes the rubber hit the road on a daily basis.

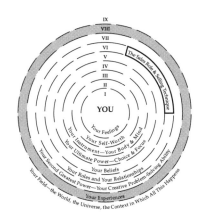

20

What Happens *Today* Makes the Difference

	Yes	*No*
1. Is it important to you to be a man or woman of action?	☐	☐
2. Would you like to know the secret to all time management systems?	☐	☐
3. Would you like to be able to engage in effective action while not losing sight of the big picture?	☐	☐

Let us assume that you are fairly well persuaded about the wisdom of having an annual plan. A good annual plan really presents a focused context within which you must execute. Execution, action, "doing" the right things on a daily basis, however, is where reality is, where achievement is, where results are brought home. The good and bad things about outside selling is that most salespeople are free to structure their day any way they want to. The achievers in selling are acutely aware of their most precious irreversible re-source—time. They know that time is designed for one thing—to do the right things. Three things are essential, then, to optimize the use of time: (1) know what the right things are, (2) know exactly when you are going to do them, and (3) do them.

Any system of time management can help you do this. But I am going to give you the system I use every day. It helps me to optimize my use of time on a regular basis, relate what I want to do to all the rings on the ripple graphic, and remember why I am on this planet. A blank form is first displayed in Figure 7. Before I get into a detailed explanation, please familiarize yourself with it. After doing that, look at the sample form that is filled out in Figure 8. The subsequent explanation of each part of it will then be much clearer.

Notice at the very top the title I gave the format, "Stay Focused!" It is a title, an admonition, a recommendation, my fondest wish, and the key to effective action. What do you focus on? You focus on the things that are really important in you life in the short and long term. What the format does is to highlight all of these goals, and the very act of highlighting them (bringing them to your conscious awareness) increases the likelihood that you will take steps to achieve them.

The top line puts the day first because it is more concrete and easier to remember than the date. It also fixes your attention on today. It is today that things, in fact, get done.

In the bold bordered rectangle are "reminders" to maintain your focus. Look at letters A and B. These remind you to take care of your instrument—your mind and your body. If they are functioning optimally, all kinds of good things can happen. If, on the other hand, you are dissipated, deenergized, unfocused, and sick, sustainable success and good feelings are not likely. These prompters remind you to just do it—the MRE, aerobic exercise, eating right, breathing right, ACE tablet, and muscle strengthening. They are the rock-bottom foundation for any personal growth program.

Letter C refers to your purpose in life. This reminds you of your basic philosophy of life, and provides the big picture that captures the meaning of it all for you. You should be able to summarize this thought in a few brief epigrammatic words, such as "Serve others"; "Help others to become happier"; "Maximize my

Figure 7. Form for staying focused (blank).

Stay Focused!

Day _____ Date _____

Reminders to Maintain My Focus

A. Mental Renewal Exercise _____ A.M. _____ P.M. _____ in between
B. Physical Renewal Practices: *aerobic exercise*—15 minutes every day, the rest of your life; *eat*—70% fruits and vegetables, watch fat intake (<25 grams); take your *ACE tablet* daily; *breathe deeply* throughout the day—diaphragmatically, and "10X = 3X"; and do your *strengthen the muscles* routine.
C. My purpose in life _____
D. What do I have to be grateful for? _____
E. Goals—key words _____

Instructions: Do the five steps below each day.

1. What action steps will I take today to accomplish objectives? *(Display the possibilities first; don't order or evaluate yet.)*

2. Check important ones and allocate a time frame.

Time Frames

6:00	_____
7:00	_____
8:00	_____
9:00	_____
10:00	_____
11:00	_____
12:00	_____
1:00	_____
2:00	_____
3:00	_____
4:00	_____
5:00	_____
6:00	_____
7:00	_____
8:00	_____
9:00	_____

To Do?

What Else?

3. What problems/obstacles stand in the way of having a great day? How can I remove them? _____
_____

4. The PFC focus

> **Person:** What can I do for my health and personal growth today? _____
> _____
>
> **Family:** How can I help _____ feel special today? _____
> _____
>
> **Career:** How can I improve my service today? _____
> _____

5. Creative ideas: What ideas might enable my company, my department, my team, or me to do more? _____
_____
_____

Notes _____
_____
_____

Figure 8. Form for staying focused (sample—filled out).

Stay Focused!

Day __Monday__   Date __August 22, 1994__

> *Reminders to Maintain My Focus*
>
> A. Mental Renewal Exercise ___6:30___ A.M. _____ P.M. _____ in between
> B. Physical Renewal Practices: *aerobic exercise*—15 minutes every day, the rest of your life; *eat*—70% fruits and vegetables, watch fat intake (<25 grams); take your *ACE tablet* daily; *breathe deeply* throughout the day—diaphragmatically, and "10X = 3X"; and do your *strengthen the muscles* routine.
> C. My purpose in life __serve while enjoying my service__
> D. What do I have to be grateful for? __family; new car; home; job; great colleagues; health__
> E. Goals—key words __vacation house; Czech trip; millionaire status; President's Club__

Instructions: Do the five steps below each day.

1. What action steps will I take today to accomplish objectives? *(Display the possibilities first; don't order or evaluate yet.)*

2. Check important ones and allocate a time frame.

Time Frames

Time	
6:00	
7:00	Exercises - Planning
8:00	
9:00	Telephone Calls
10:00	Enter Orders
11:00	Prepare presentation
12:00	Salad at Desk
1:00	
2:00	meet - F.G.
3:00	meet - S.T. presentation
4:00	meet - J.M.
5:00	interview candidate
6:00	
7:00	
8:00	Dine Out
9:00	

3. What problems/obstacles stand in the way of having a great day? How can I remove them? __Interruptions – especially Joe; only spend 1 hour in office + stand up when Joe comes in.__

4. The PFC focus
    Person: What can I do for my health and personal growth today? __Jog, MRF, Fruits + Veggies – No alcohol__
    Family: How can I help __Mary Jo__ feel special today? __Dinner tonight @ 8:00 pm · Catfish Pete's__
    Career: How can I improve my service today? __Read ½ hour - Hopkin's book__

5. **Creative ideas:** What ideas might enable my company, my department, my team, or me to do more? __Do some quantum leap thinking on Micro Mac account.__

Notes __Start thinking about the 4th quarter rush.__

good feelings"; "Make the world a better place"; "Enjoy the trip"; "Achieve enlightenment"; "Be a model of the Golden Rule." It's up to you to decide what it is, but it is useful to think about it every day, and write it out.

Letter D refers to your gratitudes. Thinking about the things you are grateful for immediately starts your day on a positive note. It is not possible to be thinking about the things you are grateful for and be depressed at the same time. The exercise is an upper, a good feeling producer, and by itself can put you into an achieving state. The state is one of hope and optimism. This is the way to proceed with your day.

Whereas letter D looks back for inspiration, letter E, "goals—key words," looks ahead. Again, the key word will carry with it all the associations you want: "vacation house," "one million net," "Czech trip," "President's Club." Line up four or five of your big goals.

Below the rectangular box is the statement "Instructions: Do the five steps below each day." Start with number one. Look at the question: "What action steps will I take today to accomplish objectives?" Notice how the "to do's" are displayed in the filled-in example. This is another use of the mind map that was discussed in Chapter 17. It is what I call getting the dump out first, without any concern about order or priority or elegance. Just get it out. Each "to do" is captured with a key word—no big explanation or description—and each is encircled with a balloon and has a string going back to the core, or back to another balloon if it is a subdivision. Once the display is out there, go to number two.

Number two: "Check important ones and allocate a time frame." These are the things you must do today. If you do this in another color, that will make it even easier to read. Once you have selected your important "to do's," the key to establishing your priority of action is to give each one of the important "to do's" a time frame. Write a key word in the time slot when you will actually do it. This is your plan of action for the day. Your goal is to follow it with precision.

Number three asks you to respond to these questions: "What problems/obstacles stand in the way of having a great day? How can I remove them?" Since many a great plan goes out the door because of interruptions or crises, see if you can anticipate the things that would prevent you from following your plan. Get creative in addressing the obstacles before they are in front of you. Plug any of these good strategies into your plan, if possible.

Number four is "the PFC focus." PFC stands for person, family, and career, the three pillars most people base their life on. Notice the question associated with each category. "Person: What can I do for my health and personal growth today?" Once again, this puts taking care of yourself back on the front burner, and challenges you to consciously think about it. A person might respond with key words like "join the health club today" or "attend lunchtime concert at the chapel" or "go vegetarian today."

Under "Family," notice the question, "How can I help _____ feel special today?" Family can be used in the broadest sense of the term, either as a metaphor or to refer to actual or potential members of your family. When I do this, I typically put my wife's name there, and ask myself, "How can I help Rosemarie feel special today?" What this does is force me to think about doing something magnanimous, generous, affectionate, to show her I care about her. I know for sure that the way to kill a relationship is to ignore the people in your life who are important. By thinking about how to make someone feel special, you increase the odds that you will do something surprising today.

The third category is "Career." Of all the things that I know about career advancement, this one question taps the greatest potential over which you have control: "How can I improve my service today?" Responding to this question every day will ignite many great ideas that can make your service better, smarter, and more effective. By enhancing your service, you will give your career a sky hook to the next level fast.

Number five taps into your creative imagination again, and prompts you to think about more ingenious ways in which you, your team, your department, or your company can do things better.

Finally, there is a section for notes. This gives you one predictable spot to jot down things you want to remember.

Using this form can take you less than ten minutes, but it can focus your entire day by giving you structure and priorities. Feel free to copy it, and make up your own binder. (Use Figure 7.) So, test it out; you will discover that you enjoy getting organized, and the payoff in improved well-being and productivity will become self-evident.

Summary and Bridge

The rubber hits the road on a day-to-day basis. If you are not focused in your behavior, you will squander resources on trivia. Your most irreversible resource, time, will slip through your hands like grains of sand, and you will come up empty. This simple form is designed to get you to say yes to your actions in a number of very specific ways. When you organize your life utilizing this form, you will discover that your control of your life and time will improve dramatically. Test it out.

The next chapter puts what you do in the context of all the things you want to do in your life, and suggests how to design a great life.

21

Power Questions to Design a Great Life

	Yes	*No*
1. Do you realize that selling is only a part of your life?	☐	☐
2. Is it important for you to get more passion and enthusiasm into your life?	☐	☐
3. Would you like to live a life about which you can be truly proud?	☐	☐

It is not enough to be great in sales, exceed all targets, and reap the monetary rewards that come with sales success. It is important to ask, What else can I do with my time and my life? The answer flows logically out of the points made in Chapter 3, where I asked you if you are a 10, if you are committed to excellence, and, if so, in terms of your special destiny, how can you make it happen? You and I know that good things do not happen consistently to a person by chance. We need to control what we can control. The best way to control anything is to have a plan. If you want to control the quality of your life, you need a plan. This chapter is a work chapter. If you want to make it work for you, and if you truly want a great life, filled with enriching experiences, adventure, fun, passion, and service, then put your pen in hand and start answering the questions below. When you have answered these questions thoroughly, you will have the secret to making your life a fulfilling, high-energy trip.

If you are in a relationship with someone else, spouse or lover (sometimes they are the same), invite that other to answer the questions independently, and then share your responses with each other. However, if you want this to be a good experience for both of you, *do not criticize* any of the dreams or goals the other has. Simply try to understand them, and adopt a posture of support, encouragement, and cooperation. Many common dreams and goals will undoubtedly surface in the process. Approach this playfully, and periodically do it in its entirety, or even in a modified manner, but commit yourself to revisiting the process *throughout the rest of your lives.*

Some questions are open-ended and require your full response if you wish to benefit. Other questions allow a yes or no response. The correct answer is always yes. With a yes, you then *do* what the questions imply.

So, begin.

I. Real Commitment to Designing a Quality Life

- Are you willing to take the steps to design a life that you know you could have? Pick up your pen!
- Are you willing to respond to all these questions in writing?
- Where will you write down the responses to all of these questions?
- Briefly, why are you on this planet?
- Briefly, what do you truly value in life, and how do you show that in your behavior?

II. Dream List

- What would you like to do? To have? To experience? To create? To achieve? To learn? Who would you like to meet? Have a better relationship with? Invite into your life? Where would you like to go? To live? To visit? How would you like

to be—Mentally? Physically? Personally? Healthwise? What
else would you like?

- What are the key target areas of your life—sectors in which
  you want to make things happen (e.g., personal growth,
  health, finances, marriage, family, education, social life, rec-
  reation, career, home, possessions)? Are there any other important areas?
- What additional dreams do you have in these key target
  areas?
- Are you willing to maintain your Dream List in writing from
  now on, and regularly add to it all those things that could
  enrich your life?

III. Make the Dream a Goal

- Are the dreams you have consistent with your ethics? Do
  they have some stretch built in? Review each one and modify
  it, if necessary.
- Are you willing to recast each dream in the following manner: "To do how much of what by when"? Do it—your
  dream list will be transformed with greater precision into a
  goal list.
- What does your goal list look like now?
- Are you willing to cut out or make pictures that either repre-
  sent or symbolize each one of your goals? Do it.
- Are you willing to paste them in your goal book? For those
  goals you are willing to go public on, are you willing to hang
  reminders of them in high-traffic areas of your home? Do it.
- Under each of your key target areas, write out one to three
  goals that are really important to you.

IV. Deepening Desire With Compelling Reasons

- For each goal, what are all the things you would gain if you
  did indeed achieve it?
- For each goal, what would you miss or lose or what would
  it cost you if you did not achieve it?
- For each goal, what resources do you have available that
  would help you achieve it? Make a resource list.

- Are you willing to write a paragraph for each goal stating why you will definitely achieve it? Do it.
- For each goal, what is the result of the "rocking chair" test? (The rocking chair test: Project yourself into old age and, looking back, consider how you will feel if you do or don't achieve the goal.)
- When you look back on your life to date, what things, big or small, have you accomplished that you are proud of? Make a Proud List.

V. Make a Plan

- For each goal, what personality attributes, behaviors, and attitudes have prevented or might prevent you from achieving it?
- For each goal, what other obstacles could prevent you from achieving it?
- What steps can you take to remove all obstacles that stand in the way of achieving each of your goals?
- For each goal, are you willing to make a written plan of action that specifies each important step you should take? (Each action step should be listed in order of execution following this familiar format: "To do how much of what by when.") Do it.
- Are you willing to plan each day of your life from now on, so that every day you make progress toward achieving your major goals? Start right now.

VI. Reinforcement

- For each goal, who could be a role model for you--someone who is already achieving what you want?
- Are you willing to find out how they did it, imitate their strategy, and periodically, in fantasy or in real life, ask them for advice?
- What reminders are you going to use to keep your priorities in front of you? Make a reminder list.
- Periodically ask yourself: "What would an ideal day look like?"
- What would a RAVE exercise (Relaxation, Affirmation, Visu-

alization, Emotionalization) look like for your most important goal?
- How can you anchor yourself into resourcefulness? Physiology? Mindset? Empowering questions?
- Are you willing to achieve sustained high energy by following the high-energy regimen?

VII. The Life Design Process

- Are you willing to put your goals and plans in writing routinely?
- Are you willing to keep a goal-setting workbook from now on?
- Are you willing to review, revise, and update your life plan weekly?
- Are you willing to do something constructive each day to progress toward your goals?
- Are you willing to make a list of all the things you are grateful for in your life, and whenever you are down, or need to be strengthened, review it?
- What are you going to do to reinforce your commitment to a quality life?
- When your life is over, what would you like carved on your tombstone (e.g., Malcolm Forbes—"When he was alive, he lived"; Don Noone—"He helped many people to be happy, and enjoyed the trip himself")?

Summary and Bridge

If you have followed through on the responses to these questions, you have, in my judgment, a tool to help you have a great life. What is implied, however, is that goal setting is a way of life, and has everything to do with ring VIII in the ripple graphic. Planning in the manner proposed here can give you maximum control of the things you do control: your time, your energy, your money, your relationships, your dreams!

The next chapter brings it all together in a simple checklist format.

22

Bringing It All Together

	Yes	No
1. Would you like to have a reminder in one place of how to achieve greatness in sales *and* greatness in life?	☐	☐
2. Is it important to you to be everything you could be?	☐	☐
3. Is it important to you to do everything you want to do?	☐	☐

Before every takeoff, an airline pilot and crew go through a checklist to make certain they have evaluated every important system in the plane. They do this in order to ensure a safe takeoff, a safe flight, and a safe landing. Since your life is the most important flight you will ever take, below is a checklist that I suggest you go through every day. It brings all the recommendations that I have made throughout this book together in one place. The checklist can remind you of what they are and, if you check no, generate a little guilt. This is what I call good guilt—a gentle prod to encourage you to get on with it and achieve the greatness to which you are summoned. If on occasion you are not able to do it, don't get stressed; simply regard the checklist as a daily ideal. Do it whenever you can, and remember, any time you do it is better than no time.

Beyond Technique Checklist

	Yes	No
1. Did you start off today by *acting* enthusiastic?	☐	☐
2. Did you reflect on the pleasures/rewards associated with achieving your goals?	☐	☐
3. Did you reflect on the pains you will experience if you don't?	☐	☐
4. Are you overcoming inertia and letting the principle of positive momentum work for you?	☐	☐
5. Are you anchoring yourself regularly with a yes!?	☐	☐
6. Are you reaffirming your 10ness each day?	☐	☐
7. Have you ceased the self-condemning judgments?	☐	☐
8. Will you do your MRE (mental renewal exercise) today?	☐	☐
9. Will you do RAVE today?	☐	☐
10. Will you do 70–30 on your eating?	☐	☐
11. Will you do 10X–3X in deep breathing today?	☐	☐
12. Will you get fifteen minutes of aerobic exercise in today?	☐	☐
13. Will you take an ACE today?	☐	☐
14. Will you do your muscle-strengthening routine today?	☐	☐
15. Are you maintaining your focus today?	☐	☐
16. Have you defined and are you continuing to define your occupation in a positive manner?	☐	☐

17. Are you acting against irrational fears? ☐ ☐
18. Are you making it impossible for yourself to fail? ☐ ☐
19. Are you getting enough noes? ☐ ☐
20. Are you letting forgiveness emancipate you from guilt and anger? ☐ ☐
21. Are you catching others doing something right, and telling them? ☐ ☐
22. Are you a model of Golden Rule communication? ☐ ☐
23. Are you improving your skill at handling manipulators? ☐ ☐
24. Are you dealing better with conflict? ☐ ☐
25. Are you applying your knowledge of negotiation? ☐ ☐
26. Are you game-free yet? ☐ ☐
27. Are you no longer getting hooked into others' games? ☐ ☐
28. Are you becoming an overflowing idea generator? ☐ ☐
29. Are you greeting problems as opportunities? ☐ ☐
30. Are you using quantum leap thinking periodically? ☐ ☐
31. Are you operating with a plan of action that has teeth? ☐ ☐
32. Are you using a daily written plan? ☐ ☐
33. Are you using the ethics check for the moral mazes? ☐ ☐
34. Have you written out your plan for creating a great life? ☐ ☐
35. Are you referring to the book *Great Sales Great Life* to remind you and reinforce all your good intentions on a regular basis? ☐ ☐
36. On a continuing basis, are you giving a yes! to yourself, your life, your experiences, your relationships, and your occupation? ☐ ☐

Conclusion

Please photocopy this checklist and use it each day. Just as the pilot uses a checklist before takeoff so as not to forget anything important, this checklist will remind you of the yeses! and many ripples that can lift you to greatness in selling and greatness in life.

Nothing in life happens until execution is begun and completed. So close on your desire, your will, your drive, your motivation, your goals, and your dreams, but most of all, close on doing. The act is the parent of the accomplishment. Let me end with my favorite refrain:

Do it!
Do it when you don't feel like it!
Do it especially when you don't feel like it!

When you do, the momentum will carry you to the next step, and the next, and the next . . . until you can have proudly chiseled on your tombstone:

_____(Your Name)_____ DID IT!

Recommended Readings

Alessandra, Tony, Gary Couture, and Gregg Baron. *The Idea-a-Day Guide to Super Selling and Customer Service*. Chicago: Dartnell, 1992.

Andreas, Steve, and Connie Andreas. *Change Your Mind and Keep the Change*. Moab, Utah: Real People Press, 1987.

Bailey, Covert. *The New Fit or Fat*. Boston: Houghton Mifflin, 1991.

Benson, Herbert. *The Relaxation Response*. New York: William Morrow & Company, 1975.

Bettger, Frank. *How I Raised Myself From Failure to Success in Selling*. New York: Prentice-Hall, 1949.

Blanchard, Kenneth and Norman Vincent Peale. *The Power of Ethical Management*. New York: William Morrow & Company, 1988.

Briggs, Dorothy Corkille. *Celebrate Yourself*. New York: Doubleday, 1977.

Chopra, Deepak. *Quantum Healing*. New York: Bantam, 1989.

Covey, Steven. *The Seven Habits of Highly Effective People*. New York: Simon & Schuster, 1989.

Dorsey, David. *The Force*. New York: Random House, 1994.

Gordon, Thomas. *Leader Effectiveness Training*. New York: Wyden, 1977.

Handler, Sheldon Saul. *The Oxygen Breakthrough*. New York: William Morrow & Company, 1989.

Hopkins, Tom. *How to Master the Art of Selling*. Scottsdale, Ariz.: Champion Press, 1980.

Jampolsky, Gerald. *Love Is Letting Go of the Fear*. New York: Bantam, 1979.

LeBoeuf, Michael. *How to Win Customers and Keep Them for Life*. New York: Putnam, 1987.

Mooney, William, and Donald J. Noone. *ASAP: The Fastest Way to*

Create a Memorable Speech. Hauppauge, New York: Barron's Educational Series, 1992.

Noone, Donald J. *Creative Problem Solving.* Hauppauge, New York: Barron's Educational Series, 1993.

Ornish, Dean. *Dr. Dean Ornish's Program for Reversing Heart Disease.* New York: Random House, 1990.

Robbins, Anthony. *Unlimited Power.* New York: Ballantine Books, 1986.

Thompson, Chic. *What a Great Idea!* New York: HarperPerennial, 1992.

Von Oech, Roger. *A Whack on the Side of the Head.* New York: Warner, 1990.

Ury, William. *Getting Past No.* New York: Bantam, 1993.

Index